Skunks, Nuts,
and Other Stories

A Chronicle Culled from the Oral Histories
of the Moore/Evans Clan

John L. Moore

SUNBURY
PRESS

Mechanicsburg, PA USA

In memory of David Evan Moore

1977 – 1990

Contents

Introduction

WHERE WOULD WE BE without stories? By telling stories about ourselves and our families, we make sense of our lives, we recognize patterns, see folly repeated, lessons learned, dreams realized, discoveries made. By understanding our family's past, we develop a greater sense of self and how we came to be who we are. Choices made by our relatives and ancestors and the stories about them that have been passed down through generations—whether humorous or heart wrenching—enrich our lives. They bear witness to those who came before us. The dead, momentarily, come alive. And by telling these stories, we, too, become a link in this great genealogical chain.

Carefully transcribed and supplemented with meticulous historical research, the oral histories collected here cover over two hundred years of American history. From the Revolutionary War to the 1836 Battle of the Alamo, on to the Civil War, through the Great Depression and the Cold War, the Civil Rights movement of the 1960s, and into the 21st century. You'll find Moore and Evans men fighting wars, boys playing pranks, a brother and sister watching the sky for Charles Lindbergh's "The Spirit of St. Louis," women voting for the first time after the ratification of the 19th Amendment, a mother inventing an inflatable wading pool . . . and many more anecdotes that capture defining and memorable moments.

The oral histories in John L. Moore's **Skunks, Nuts, and Other Stories** are testimony to the lives of those who the stories are about, to those who tell them, and to all the Moores and Evanses who are closely or distantly related. And beyond the Moore and Evans clans, these oral histories form a family legacy that is an important part of our collective cultural history.

I know the author of this book; he's my brother-in-law. I knew his mother, the Queen of Scrabble. I knew the dying boy—John's son—who wanted the scariest Halloween mask imaginable, perhaps because he wanted to scare the dickens out of everybody else, just as he himself was scared. Some of these stories made me laugh, others made me cry, and that's the best read, I think: personal stories that embrace both the levity and gravity of life.

~ Sara Pritchard, author of the linked-story collections *Crackpots* and *Help Wanted: Female*

Whatever happened to Grandfather's Civil War rifles?

THE CIVIL WAR SOLDIER at the core of this story was a young Pittsburgh, Pennsylvania, man, Frederick Bennett, who enlisted in the Union Army in September 1864.

Family legends told and retold by Bennett's descendants had him captured in a battle somewhere Down South and held as a POW at Andersonville, a notorious Confederate prison in Georgia.

The truth, as I learned not long ago, is much less glamorous. Bennett, who eventually became the maternal grandfather of my maternal grandfather, spent most of his nine months as a soldier on guard duty in and around Washington, D.C. For a short period of time, as General Philip Sheridan led Northern soldiers up and down the Shenandoah Valley in late 1864, Bennett's regiment guarded a strategic railroad line in Virginia. The army used this railroad to ship supplies to Sheridan's soldiers as they fought the Rebels and destroyed farms up and down the Shenandoah.

Thus far, I haven't uncovered any evidence that my ancestor ever fired a shot at an enemy soldier or was ever shot at. However, it appears that when the war ended in 1865, Bennett took two Civil War rifles back to Pittsburgh.

Many Union soldiers used muskets, which had smooth barrels. In contrast, the inside of a rifle barrel had special grooves, or rifling, that made the bullet spin at a tremendous speed when it left the barrel. A spinning bullet fired by a rifle could travel farther with greater accuracy than could a musket ball fired by a gun with a smooth bore.

To be perfectly clear, the weapons that figure in this story were rifles, not muskets.

By the mid-1920s, Frederick Bennett had passed on, and the rifles had been passed down to his grandson, Harry Evans Sr., a Pittsburgh pharmacist employed by a company that owned a chain of drug stores and was going through a period of expansion. The company assigned Evans to open a store in Cleveland, a promotion that prompted him to move his family from Pittsburgh.

Evans, who was my grandfather, was very proud of his Civil War heirlooms, which he kept in the basement. Even so, he sometimes let his sons, John and Harry Jr., play with the weapons, provided the guns weren't loaded.

One rainy Sunday, John and Harry Jr. looked forward to an afternoon of boredom. As the family ate dinner, John said to Harry, "It's too bad we can't go down to the cellar after dinner, and play with the Civil War rifles."

"Yes," Harry replied. "It is too bad we can't go down to the cellar after dinner and play with the Civil War rifles."

This exchange caught their father's attention, and he asked, "Well, boys. Why can't you go downstairs after dinner and play with those old rifles?"

"Because," the boys said, "when we moved from Pittsburgh last spring, Mother gave them to the moving men."

The roar that erupted from their father's mouth must have been nearly as loud as the cannon fire at Gettysburg.

The irate man angrily rebuked his wife, and she blasted him back.

"Those two could really go at it," Uncle Harry said with a chuckle. He said that after the fireworks died down, his father didn't speak a word to his mother for at least six weeks.

More than 75 years later, Uncle Harry told me all about that long-ago Sunday afternoon. Our talk took place on Harry's 90th birthday in 2003. He was a marvelous storyteller with a sharp memory, and I made lots of notes as he spoke.

I often watch *Antiques Roadshow* on public television, and from time to time, someone invariably brings in a Civil War musket or rifle for an appraisal. In one episode a few years ago, the expert told a man that his old rifle was worth at least $15,000.

I'm waiting for the program in which somebody shows up with a pair of Civil War rifles. I anticipate that when the appraiser asks how the weapons came into the family, the person replies, "Oh, my grandfather helped a family move from Pittsburgh to Cleveland back in the 1920s, and the woman gave him the rifles."

They were hanging Emily's diapers when Charles Lindbergh flew by

TWO EVENTS OCCURRED in 1927.

The first occurred at 7:52 a.m. on May 20 near Garden City, Long Island, as Charles Lindbergh piloted the Spirit of St. Louis, with its 200-horsepower engine, down the runway at Roosevelt Field. He was headed for France.

Nobody had ever flown across the Atlantic Ocean non-stop, but the Lone Eagle's single-engine monoplane did the distance—3,610 miles— in 33 hours and 32 minutes.

Lindbergh's accomplishment grabbed headlines around the globe, but the world hardly noticed the second event, the birth of a baby girl named Emily on June 5 in East Liverpool, Ohio. Emily was the youngest of five children. Her parents were Florence and Harry Evans Sr.

Emily's two oldest siblings, 13-year-old Harry and Virginia, who was 12, were old enough to share in the national excitement that Lindbergh created. They were also old enough to help their mother perform some of the drudgery associated with having babies back then—washing cloth diapers and then hanging them out on the line to dry.

Suddenly famous as the Lone Eagle, the 25-year-old Lindbergh returned to the U.S., then took the Spirit of St. Louis on a 22,000-mile victory flight to all 48 states. His three-month tour began July 20 and took him to more than 80 cities. One leg of the tour took him over East Liverpool, where Virginia, Harry, Emily and the other Evanses lived in a rented two-story wood frame house.

One evening in late July, Harry and Virginia were visiting a neighboring family that had a radio. Everybody got excited when a newscaster reported that the Lone Eagle would fly from nearby Pittsburgh to Cleveland the next day. It was possible, they thought, that Lindbergh's plane might fly over their community since it was on the way to Cleveland.

Virginia and Harry were so enthusiastic that when they went home, "we spent the rest of the night listening to my brother's crystal set, which I wasn't allowed to touch," said Virginia, who was an octogenarian when I collected this story. "We had a set of headphones" for listening to the crystal set, and "Harry put it on my head and then he took it off."

The brother and sister may have had their heads high in the clouds as they dreamed of becoming daring aviators, but the next morning their mother brought them down to earth.

"Mother said, 'I have a lot of work to do with the new baby, and you two can help by hanging up the diapers.' She took us out in the yard, and showed us exactly how to hang them," Virginia said.

There were lots of diapers, and Virginia and Harry weren't exactly thrilled at the prospect of spending a good deal of the morning hanging them on the clothesline, especially when they could have been keeping a lookout for Charles Lindbergh.

There were lots and lots of diapers, and the morning passed slowly. It was nearly lunchtime when the last diaper was pinned and hanging on the rope.

Virginia's memory is clear on what happened next.

"Harry said, 'Keep your eyes on the sky because it's time for Charles Lindbergh to come over. He's

7

due to come by at 12 o'clock, and it's just about 12 now.'"

Suddenly they heard the sound of the engine of a distant airplane.

And then they saw a single-engine, silver-gray monoplane heading their way.

"We looked up, and here comes a plane," Virginia said. "We were so excited. We jumped up and down and we screamed, 'Lucky Lindy! Up in the Sky.'

"It was a bright sunny morning, and as the plane passed overhead, there was 'a great deal of reflection' from the plane's metal fuselage," Virginia said.

They could see some writing on the plane: " Spirit of St. Louis," but the plane was too far away for them to see Lindbergh himself.

Then something happened that neither child ever forgot. As Lindbergh passed overhead, the shadow of the Spirit of St. Louis crossed their yard. "We stepped in the shadow of the plane," Virginia said.

After that, "We ran into the house and called our mother," Virginia said.

The Evans children could hardly wait until the local newspaper arrived. The aviator was hot news, and the editors had included a story about his Pittsburgh-Cleveland trip.

"It was headlines," Virginia said. "I remember spreading the newspaper out on the floor and reading everything it said."

Nuts!

THIS IS A STORY written by an old man attempting to remember one of the stories that he heard as a boy, a tale that his father liked to tell about an adventure he had as a boy. Dad always laughed and smiled as he told this story, which, at its core, detailed juvenile disappointment, resilience, and defiance. I strive not to embellish the story, but to lay it out as accurately, colorfully and mirthfully as I heard it told some 60 years ago.

Leon H. Moore Jr. was my father. Willis S. Moore was his younger brother. They grew up in a two-story wood frame house on Cottage Hill in Lambertville, New Jersey. My grandparents lived there until 1948, and my family used to go there on visits from Somerville, which was about 25 miles away. I remember that our car, which was black with shiny chrome, strained a bit to climb the street to their house, which was a faded blue. My grandmother kept a flower garden with tall irises, which were blue. There was an outhouse – a one-seater with an awful odor – a short distance (30 feet perhaps) beyond the kitchen door. My grandfather, Leon H. Sr., had been a carpenter, but had fallen and broken his back. In time, the fractures healed, and he could stand upright and walk without limping, but after the injury he didn't work, and my grandmother, Mary, had earned money by doing wash for other families on Cottage Hill. So my mother said.

The Moores of 1917 had a vegetable garden, and the boys caught fish and turtles in the summer time, and, armed with air rifles, shot rabbits and squirrels in the fall. They brought their catch and quarry home, and their mother cooked and served it. The boys had a much younger sister, Mary, but she rarely figured in any of the stories. (About the only one I recall is that Dad once said Willis used to make Mary wait on him, and that Dad once gave Willis a poke in an effort to make him stop.)

One Saturday morning in late October, circa 1917, the boys went out in the woods at the edge of town to gather hickory nuts. I reconstruct the date, picturing Dad, who had chestnut hair and big ears that stood out, as about 12. Willis would have been 9 or 10. They knew a grove of hickory trees a distance off a dirt farm lane. There weren't any paths leading through or past this grove, which they had discovered one day while out shooting squirrels. When they told their mother they intended to gather hickory nuts, she gave them a large cloth sack. Air rifles in hand, they descended Cottage Hill on the run. It was a frosty morning, and their breath turned white as it hit the air.

The boys spent the morning happily scouring the grove for hickory nuts, slowly filling the bag. They grew hungry as lunchtime approached, and started out for home. They made their way through the brush and at length came to the lane that led to town. They were pleased with the morning's enterprise and took turns carrying the cloth sack. As they walked they heard the whinny of a horse coming up behind them. They turned and saw a wagon driven by the farmer who lived at the end of the lane. The farmer overtook them, and they waved and greeted him even though he wasn't known as a friendly man.

The farmer stopped the wagon. "Morning, boys," he said. "What do you have in that bag?"

"Nuts," Leon said.

"We spent all morning gathering them," Willis said.

"What kind of nuts, boys?"

"Hickory nuts," Leon said.

"Where'd you find them, boys?"

"In those woods," Leon said, pointing toward the grove of hickory trees.

"Who owns those woods?" the man asked.

"We don't know," Willis said.

"I do. That's my land over there," the farmer said.

The boys hadn't considered that somebody might own those woods, and they accepted the farmer's word.

"Well, boys. If I own those hickory trees, then I guess I own those hickory nuts. Give me the bag."

Stunned, the boys didn't respond.

"Come on, boys. They're my nuts. Give me the bag."

Reluctantly, Leon handed the sack to the farmer.

"Thanks," the farmer said without smiling. With that, he picked up the reins, said "giddy up" to his horse, a spirited chestnut stallion, and continued on his way to Lambertville.

The exchange angered the boys. "Mean son of a bitch," Leon muttered when the man had gone too far away to hear.

The wagon moved around a bend and out of view, and the boys resumed their walk home. The bounce was gone from their step, and their faces wore unhappy expressions. They knew they would never get the hickory nuts back.

Back home, their mother made lunch for them. They ate quickly and quietly, and didn't reply when she asked what was wrong.

When they finished, they went to their room and got their BB guns and a handful of pellets. They started to laugh and run – and headed back to the woods.

"Do you think the farmer has come back from town yet?" Willis asked.

"I hope not," Leon said.

They scampered down the lane, then slowed to a deliberate walk. Their eyes scanned the brush lining the road, which ran nearly straight for about a mile along the foot of the hillside, then made a sharp turn around an outcropping of boulders.

"Look," Leon said. "There's a big tree that the wind knocked down."

"Yeah," Willis said, smiling. "We can hide behind that."

"Yep," Leon said.

"How long you think we have to wait?"

"An hour maybe."

The boys positioned themselves behind the tree, which shielded them from view from the lane. As it happened that day, Willis and Leon were wearing jackets and clothes that had drab colors, and their natural coloring and their brown jackets and dark pants blended well with the foliage of the autumn woods. The farmer wouldn't be looking for youngsters lying in wait, and their clothes wouldn't give them away.

As if they were soldiers in the infantry, they lay in prone positions behind the tree, with their BB guns pointed toward the lane. The boulders blocked their view of the lane's straight stretch, so they watched – and listened – vigilantly. Eventually they heard the clip clop, clip clop of the horse's easy gait. A minute later the horse, wagon and farmer came into view.

The boys felt a rush of adrenaline as they peered through the brush. They aimed their BB guns, and waited, wondering if their nerve would fail. Originally they had thought to shoot at the farmer, but as the horse and wagon approached, they saw that the horse blocked their view of the man. Suddenly the horse came even with them. Indeed, it was only six or seven feet away. The boys saw its shoulder rather than its head, and then it walked right past them, presenting its soft underbelly. As its hind quarters came up, the Moore boys opened fire.

Stung by the BBs, the stallion screamed, reared and started to run down the lane. The startled farmer yelled "Whoa!" and pulled hard on the reins, but failed to bring horse under control. The Moore boys said later that they came out from their hiding place and laughed as they watched the horse take the farmer on a wild ride down the lane toward his farm. Then the horse rounded another bend, and farmer, wagon and horse sped out of view.

"Nuts," Leon said with a smile.

Willis repeated, "Nuts."

They laughed and, carrying their BBs, began to run home.

More than half a century has passed since I last heard my father tell this tale. It was one of his favorites. I don't remember whether, in Dad's telling, the farmer had a name. My sense is that the man was simply The Farmer. I picture a man in late middle-age with a stern, clean-shaven face. He probably wore an old hat or cap, a wool jacket and dark trousers. His face sported a mean-spirited smile when he reached out to confiscate the bag of hickory nuts.

Nor do I know with any certainty that the horse was a chestnut. I am sure, however, that the farmer rode in a one-horse conveyance. It's possible that his vehicle was a carriage rather than a wagon. A carriage would be lighter than a wagon – and would have been swifter on the final phase of the farmer's trip from town, but in my memory, I hear my father saying wagon. I am also certain that the horse was a stallion, not a mare. After all, this anatomical fact is basic to the climax of the piece.

I was little, no more than seven or eight, when I first heard this story. In my innocence, I failed to grasp why the horse had reacted so forcefully when the BBs hit him. I asked Dad to explain, but don't know if he gave me an explicit answer. It took time –

years, probably – but eventually, I figured it out. That's why this yarn has a title of only one word, "Nuts."

Leon died in 1960; Willis, in 1979.

December 1776:
British troops gave chase as
Charlie ran up the hill

These are the times that try men's souls.
~ Thomas Paine, December 23, 1776

ONE OF MY ANCESTORS – Charles Pidcock, a 20-year-old member of the New Jersey militia – was neither a summer soldier nor a sunshine patriot. Indeed, he was hardly on friendly terms with the British troopers who stormed his parents' house late one afternoon in December 1776.

Known around town as Charley, the militiaman was a son of Jonathan Pidcock. In the years before the American Revolution, Jonathan had acquired and operated a grist mill, a store and a small fleet of Durham boats on the Delaware River at Lambertville, then called Coryell's Ferry.

Farmers brought their grains to the mill, which ground them into flour. Charley and his brother Emanuel used the boats to ship the flour and fresh produce downriver to market in Philadelphia. They purchased merchandise that they brought upriver on the return trip, and their father sold it in his store. Boats of this type were common sights on the river during this era.

By mid-1776, father and sons belonged to a Hunterdon County company of the New Jersey militia.

Because his father wasn't physically able to bear arms, Charley sometimes marched in his father's place. But Jonathan, who was 47 and a resident of Amwell Township, still had plenty to do for The American Cause. According to "History of Amwell," Jonathan served on a Committee of Safety, which determined who was a patriot and who was a loyalist. At one point, he also served on a Committee of Inquisition that weighed the case of a man named Joseph Smith. Smith, who had lived in the township, had enlisted in the British army. It seems that the committee ordered the confiscation of Smith's property.

The Cause took a serious turn for the worse during the closing months of 1776. Following a series of defeats, General George Washington evacuated New York, and the British and Hessian soldiers chased him and his army southwest across New Jersey. In early December, it took Washington five days to move his men, horses, provisions and artillery over the Delaware and into Pennsylvania.

In a defensive move, the Americans collected all the boats they could find for many miles north and south of Trenton, and hid them behind an island along the river's west shore. Family memory is silent on this point, but, presumably, the Pidcock boats were among them.

Without boats, the Hessians and the British couldn't cross the river and come after them. At least, not until the river froze over. When that happened, the enemy soldiers could walk across.

Prior to Washington's retreat across the Jerseys, Charley had been posted in East Jersey near Elizabethtown, only a few miles from Staten Island, where the British had stationed thousands of troops.

When the Continental Army sought refuge along the Delaware, Charley went to his parents' house to rest up because his feet were extremely sore from "hard marching." Situated along the road to

Trenton, the house stood at the foot of a steep hill called Goat Hill.

Late one afternoon, Charley was at home in his stocking feet when a British patrol came up the river road from Trenton, hunting for rebels. Accompanied by Tories, they naturally stopped at the Pidcock house. After all, father and sons belonged to the militia and the father served on the Committee of Safety.

New Jersey historian James Snell in an 1881 book told what Charley did next:

"He tried to escape by the front door, but that was guarded. He went to the back door, and there too stood two armed men, but, taking advantage of the darkness, he sprang past the guard and fled up the steep sides of Goat Hill, the rocks cutting his feet at every step. A sharp volley of balls fell around him, and the soldiers rushed up the hill after him."

Charley had an advantage because he knew the terrain – and knew that there was a large rock on the hilltop. He found it in the darkness and hid behind it. "His pursuers even stood upon it, but failing to find him gave up the search," Snell reported.

At some point Charley decided it was safe to go home, and descended the hill. As he did so, he found a hat that a British officer had lost. It was a tall hat, decorated with feathers, and Charley kept it as a trophy.

Decades later, one of his fellow militiamen, George Bake, recalled: "An officer lost his hat and feathers, and Charley got it, and brought (it) over to camp the next day."

In late December, as the Americans made a surprise attack on Trenton, a nor'easter was crossing New Jersey. "Sleet and rain were falling heavily . . ., with intervals of heavy rain," reported author David Hackett Fisher in his 2004 book, *Washington's Crossing*.

Early in the morning on the day after Christmas, Charley's militia company left Coryell's Ferry and began the 16-mile march downriver to Trenton. In all likelihood, they knew that Washington had crossed the Delaware and was also heading for Trenton.

Charley and his fellows were on the outskirts of town "when we heard the firing at Trenton," George Bake recalled. The company was still en route a little later "when we heard that the Hessians were taken."

If Charley and his comrades arrived too late to fight at Trenton, they were in plenty of time for the Battle of Princeton a week later. Charley's official service record also credits him with participation there and in the October 1777 Battle of Germantown, near Philadelphia.

By late 1777, Charley had given up the soldier's life, married a young woman named Martha Hoagland, settled down and soon after started raising a family. In time, Charley and Martha became the great-grandparents of my great-grandmother, Emma Moore.

Nobody in the family seems to know whatever happened to the British officer's hat.

Big sister always sent her little brother to the front door

THE TOOLS THAT 19-year-old Virginia Evans of Pittsburgh, Pennsylvania, used to survive the Great Depression included a pound of butter, a bottle of vanilla, and her little brother.

Virginia's mother had died, and the teenager had to work in order to help support her family. When she could, she worked in downtown Pittsburgh at Kaufmann's Department Store, which hired many of its salespeople on a day-to-day basis.

That meant Virginia — and everybody else hoping to earn a day's pay — had to arrive at the store early in the morning, place her name on the list of available workers, and then join all the other would-be workers sitting in a special room where they waited for their names to be called.

Most days, the personnel office had filled all the openings by late morning. Too often, Virginia wasn't selected. "If they didn't need you," she said, "at about 11 o'clock, they sent you home."

At home, "I was my own employer. I had a cookie business in my own kitchen. If I didn't get on at Kaufmann's by 11:30, I took the closest road home."

Her younger siblings, John and Emily, would be waiting.

Starting from scratch, they would make up to ten dozen vanilla cookies. They would mix the ingredients — vanilla, white flour, white sugar and a pound of butter. "We didn't use eggs," which cost too much. "We made drop cookies. To cut them out took too much time."

The Evans children baked the cookies in the oven. The process took about "an hour from start to finish, and then we had to go out and sell them."

They walked the streets of Pittsburgh and carried the cookies in a basket. "We sold what we could ..... . We went knocking on doors."

Some people would buy a dozen cookies, others a half dozen, and some would only buy one or two. "We sold them what they could afford."

Although Virginia didn't remember the exact prices that she and her siblings charged, she said that most customers paid in nickels and dimes; transactions involving folding money were rare.

Many times, they sold the entire inventory quickly, and went home and baked another batch.

Sister Emily and brother John nearly always went along and helped sell the cookies. "She liked to carry the basket and he liked to ring the doorbells. I was there to see that nobody ate the cookies.... . . We took some water with us to drink and we figured out the route we would take ..... . We kept on until the cookies were all sold, and when they were all sold, we could go home."

Of course, the youngsters couldn't resist the tempting aroma wafting from the cookie-laden basket. "We were allowed to eat a few cookies while we were out, but we weren't supposed to eat too many."

As big-sister-in-charge, Virginia also kept the money. "Sometimes, I'd go home with my pockets filled with coins."

The money was important. During the early 1930s, there were many days when the cash the children raised by selling cookies bought groceries for the Evans family. The children knew they depended on their little business for food, and "they were so proud of what they were doing."

Their mother had died in 1930, and their father, a college graduate, was a pharmacist, but he was often unemployed during this time. "If we hadn't had a depression, he would have had a good job," Virginia remarked.

A younger sister, Mary Elizabeth, lived with relatives in Altoona during this time. An older brother, Harry, had a job selling photographs as an on-the-road salesman. "He never spent the money that he made on the road. He either brought it home or sent it home."

Cash was hard to come by, and the family guarded it carefully.

"We spent what we needed for groceries, and we would put the rest in the bank," Virginia said. Sometimes, the family had to use some of the money for shoes or some other necessity.

Before spending anything on groceries, "we always put the money aside for ingredients for the next batch."

But Virginia made more money by working at the department store than she did by selling cookies. On weekday mornings, she would rise early and head for Kaufmann's, hoping to be hired for the day. "If I were lucky, I could sell shoes or any kind of clothing," she said.

If she didn't get picked, she'd hurry home and whip up another batch of cookies.

"Long after I got married and moved away, people would knock on the door and ask if the cookie lady lived there," she said.

The Evans children survived the depression, grew up, and raised families of their own.

Harry's assignment – Find the prettiest girls in town

WHEN HARRY EVANS came into town, he had only thing on his mind – good-looking women.

"Who's the prettiest girl in town?" Harry would ask. Then he would look her up and talk her into having her picture taken.

It was 1935, and Harry, who was in his early 20s, was a traveling salesman, an agent for a Pittsburgh photography company that sent sales crews out to every nook and cranny of Pennsylvania.

Harry, who grew up in Pittsburgh, had fond memories of the year he spent working West Milton, Duncannon, Liverpool, Ashland, Mount Carmel and countless Pennsylvania towns that were too small to have a photography studio of their own.

Harry and the people he worked for had learned that men weren't particularly interested in having their photos taken, but the women were. So Harry and his colleagues sought them out and sold them coupons that were good for a photo sitting and a large sepia-tone photograph that came in a glass frame.

A ticket cost a good deal of money – $1.95.

To be sure, if a man wanted to sit for a photo, Harry would happily sell him the ticket. But women, especially younger ones in their late teens and early 20s, were much more enthusiastic.

Knowing this, Harry tracked down the blonde who had won the summer's beauty contest or the redhead or brunette who had been elected harvest queen. Whoever she was, she often liked his offer so much that she encouraged all her friends to have their pictures taken as well.

Harry and a second salesman also worked the local apparel factories where many workers were women. They arranged to arrive the day after payday when people would have money. Harry would jump up on a table and make an impromptu sales pitch "about how nice they were going to look in their new photograph." The second salesman would collect the cash for the photo coupons.

Business was brisk although, as Harry said, "we were selling a luxury when people didn't have anything to eat."

Here's how it worked: The sales crew devoted Monday and Tuesday to selling coupons. On Wednesday all the customers came down to the local hotel where the first-floor samples room had been converted into a temporary photo studio. A professional photographer arrived and spent the day taking pictures. When the shutter clicked for the last time, the film was rushed to Pittsburgh where employees of the photo company developed it, made proof sheets, and hurried the proofs back to West Milton or wherever.

This was done as rapidly as possible so that on Friday or Saturday, all the women could troop back into the hotel and select the picture they liked best. Of course, they were all encouraged to order extra prints for a grandmother, a favorite aunt and uncle – and for the boyfriend.

Once they ordered the extra prints, Harry urged them to purchase extra frames as well. The photos were an odd size – seven inches by ten inches, and "that meant they could not buy the frame in a five and dime."

A few days later, the customers would receive the photographs and frames.

In a good week, Harry earned $30 or more in commissions. He pocketed a dollar of every $1.95 ticket he sold, then passed the remaining 95 cents along to his employer. He also kept a share of the money the people spent to buy extra prints and frames.

Though some weeks were lean, Harry ordinarily made enough money to pay for his room and board in the owner-operated hotels that every small town seemed to have. He often had enough cash left over to send back to Pittsburgh where a younger sister, Virginia, cared for a brother and a sister who were even younger.

Did any of these sales situations ever lead to romantic encounters? The question prompted a smile, but Harry ducked the question and remarked that working these little towns was always very tiring.

When the week was over, the townspeople had ordered their photographs, the local hotel had earned extra revenue by providing meals and rooms to the sales gang, and Harry and his colleagues had their commissions.

"Everybody went home happy," Harry said.

The sales crew, of course, would move on to the next town, and Harry Evans would soon find himself looking for good-looking women.

The first day that women could vote

THIS IS A STORY that Virginia Evans Moore told to her children and grandchildren so many times that some of them know it by heart.

It is deeply personal, as family stories often are, but it's historic as well, for it chronicles one family's experience on the first day that American women could vote.

It takes place in 1920 when the Evans family lived on Clemesha Avenue in Pittsburgh's Brookline section. The father, Harry Sr., was a pharmacist, and the mother, Florence, was a nurse. They had three children and often employed a housekeeper.

Theirs was a fashionable, modern family. At a time when most people walked or relied on public transportation, "we always had a car," said Harry Jr., who had turned seven that August.

"We had an Overland," added Virginia, a younger sister who was not quite six.

The third child, John, was still a baby.

Mrs. Evans had long brown hair, but when fashions changed and the bob became popular, "she cut it off," Virginia said. "My father took one look at her, and he shook his head. I can hear her telling people, 'He had a fit. He acted as if it was his hair that was cut off.'"

The 19th Amendment to the U.S. Constitution was ratified in August 1920, and that gave Florence Evans and millions of other American women the right to vote. Memory grows murky with age, but

Virginia, who told me this story during an interview when she was 85, retained detailed recollections of that long-ago event.

She said that when election day approached, Mrs. Evans explained to her children that many women were going to exercise their new right "and I am, too."

As Mrs. Evans served supper one night, she announced that when the meal was over, she was going to vote and that the whole family was going with her. Excited, the children finished the meal in a hurry.

Virginia recalled that her father and mother put all three children in the backseat of the family's touring car and drove to the polling place.

They arrived at the Brookline Elementary School, which Harry and Virginia attended, and there were many women – and some men – going in to vote. "It must have been about 7 o'clock," Virginia said.

Both parents had dressed up for the occasion. Her father wore a suit and a hat, and her mother "was wearing a brown suit coat with a corsage at her neck."

Virginia and the other children stayed outside with their father. It was a clear, cool autumn night, "but it wasn't freezing."

Despite their excitement, they waited patiently for their mother. "She went in and came out, and she was like a princess. She was so happy, and my father went over and gave her a big kiss."

Virginia said that when the family returned home, Mrs. Evans telephoned many of her friends. "I can hear her saying, 'Did you vote? Did you vote?' And 90 percent of them said 'no.'"

Even though she was only five, Virginia Evans never forgot that night. It was important because "now my mother could vote. To our family that was a very big deal."

More than half a century later, when her granddaughter was as old as Virginia had been in

1920, grandmother told granddaughter how excited she had been when everybody piled into the touring car, rode to the school and watched their mother walk into the poll.

The granddaughter said that as her grandmother finished the story, "she pointed at me, and she said, 'Someday you'll vote too.'"

And she has.

The neighborhood radical
taught women to drive

A WHITE-HAIRED elderly lady sits in a wheelchair in a sunny room with some other residents of the nursing home.

The octogenarian is my mother, Virginia Evans Moore, and when we visit, we tend to talk about the good old days.

Sometimes she thinks I am her father, Harry Sr., or her brother, Harry Jr., but then I tell her that I'm her son John, and she smiles.

That's how our conversation started the other morning. It was a bright sunny day, and we got to talking about the women she once taught to drive automobiles. My mother, you see, was one of the first women to drive. Early on, my Dad had taught her.

"How long ago that was!" Mom said.

At first, her memories were fragmentary but she soon warmed up, and, revving up in high gear, she started on a verbal cruise down memory lane.

I was taking notes, and sometimes her sentences came so fast that I had to read them back. Occasionally she'd correct me.

Mom grew up in Pittsburgh and was in her early 20s when she married a New Jerseyan, Leon H. Moore Jr. The newlyweds moved to Central New Jersey in the late 1930s.

Not long after that, my father taught her to drive. "We always had a Chevy," Mom said.

Driving was something that Mom's mother, who had been both a feminist and a suffragette, had never learned, but it certainly suited the young bride.

"I drove every place you could drive a car," she said.

One summer she and her teenage sister Emily, who had lived with Mom and Dad, drove from New Jersey to Pittsburgh. The tires on their car had blowouts, and the travelers had many adventures. They returned to New Jersey with stories about a new turnpike that Pennsylvania was building across the Allegheny Mountains.

"Every road we took was under construction," Mom said.

Back then, few women drove, and in Mom's own circle of friends, "I was the only one."

It was an era when many women depended on their husbands for transportation. Mom said that if husbands didn't want their wives to go shopping, they just refused to take them.

"If they didn't have any way to go (downtown), they were house-bound," she said.

When friends and acquaintances remarked Mom was fortunate that her husband allowed her to drive, she often responded by offering to give them driving lessons.

Surprisingly, many declined. "Lots of women were afraid to learn – to step away from the house," Mom said. "It was a screwy time."

"One woman said I was lucky I could drive. I said, 'There's no reason you can't learn', but she said, 'Me? Learn to drive?' She had no confidence in herself."

Others, however, readily accepted her free lessons, which weren't complete until the learner had obtained a driver's license.

From the late 1930s through the early 1950s, Mom taught about a dozen women the skill of driving an automobile.

"That was my secret hobby," she told me.

One of her first students "had a wonderful husband . . . He was a cattle buyer, and he drove a truck," Mom said.

When the man took the truck to work, the family car sat at home in the drive. "Her husband wouldn't allow her to drive it. She might have an accident and get killed."

Mom taught the man's wife to drive anyway.

The woman didn't tell her husband, but "one day they both came to the intersection at the same time," Mom said. "I wasn't in the car at the time."

The next time the man saw Mom, he wasn't a bit shy about expressing his displeasure.

"I can still see him shaking his finger at me," she said.

Another woman, Betty, was married to a professional man who owned two black sedans. The man drove one to work, and let the second one sit in the driveway, which was black-topped. They lived in a white Cape Cod down the block from us.

Betty liked the driving lessons, but feared that her husband would find out. To prevent this, she made little chalk marks where the tires touched the macadam.

"I remember how she would have a piece of chalk in her pocket," Mom said. "When we came back, she got the tires back on the very spot so her husband wouldn't know she had had the car out."

Eventually, "her husband found out, and he never spoke to me again," Mom said. Irate, "he sold the car so she wouldn't have a car to drive."

My father was well aware that not all the husbands of Mom's student drivers appreciated the lessons my mother taught them.

"A lot of men were mad at me," Mom said with a smile.

As for my father, "he got a big charge out of that."

My mother insisted that it was important for a woman to be able to get in the car, put the key in the ignition, start the engine, drive down the street, and go where she wanted to go.

"Her whole life changed when she learned to drive," Mom said.

Mom's own life certainly changed. A high school dropout, she was in her late 30s when she drove to night courses at Somerville High School and obtained her high school equivalency certificate.

After that, she drove to Douglass College in New Brunswick five and six days a week for four years and obtained a bachelor's degree. Then she drove off to graduate school and got her master's. I know. I was there, first as a young teenager and later as a young adult, and I saw her do it.

Mom was a trail blazer.

Christmas memory: Tot's illness prompted cross-country train trip

At Christmastime, I rarely walk past a Salvation Army kettle without emptying my pocket of change or dipping into the folding money in my wallet. Highly personal feelings of gratitude and obligation prompt me to do this.

December 1947 was a difficult month for my family. My father, a robust man in his early 40s, was an electrician who worked in a plastics factory called Bakelite. My mother, a 33-year old brunette with a pleasant smile, was a full-time housewife and mother of three, one of whom was chronically ill. At five, I was the oldest, a tow-headed Kindergartener. My brother and sister, Donald and Dorothy, twins, were not quite two.

My parents were hard-working people: they had a mortgage on a modest single-family house. Dad drove a second-hand car and did all the mechanical work himself. He worked part-time as a gunsmith. A self-employed seamstress, Mom used an old sewing machine to earn pocket money.

We lived in New Jersey, and my sister had been ill for a long time. One day in early December, our family doctor told my mother that my sister's respiratory system had taken a very serious turn for the worse. "Drop everything," the doctor told mother, "and take the child to Arizona, where the drier climate might help her."

In no uncertain terms, the doctor told Mom that she and my sister needed to leave for Arizona immediately. "Don't delay," he said. "Get on a train tomorrow."

Chronically pinched for funds, my parents could hardly afford such a trip. After all, Phoenix, Ariz., was 2,400 miles away, and just the cost of a round-trip train ticket must have seemed out of reach, but Mom called the Salvation Army. Whoever took her call was sympathetic, asked many questions about my sister's illness and the family's situation, and promised to call back in a while.

The only telephone in our house was black, and it sat on a little wooden stand in the living room. When you picked it up, an operator said, "Number please." Then she placed the call for you.

The phone rang a few hours later. It was a man from the Salvation Army calling to say the trip to Arizona was all arranged and paid for. In the morning, Mom and Dorothy needed to arrive at the Pennsylvania Railroad station in New Brunswick, about 14 miles away. Periodically, physicians would meet the train to check on the child. Housing had been arranged in Arizona. Someone would meet them in New Brunswick with tickets and other information.

This conversation must have taken place on a Monday evening, because the trip would take three days, and a pediatrician had agreed to see the child in Phoenix on Friday morning.

I recall none of these details first-hand, but I know the story by heart. Dad drove Mom and Dorothy to the station in the family's old Chevy, a black four-door sedan. The Salvation Army representative handed the tickets along with a thick envelope to my mother, who cried as she kissed my father goodbye. Dad was a rugged, no-nonsense outdoorsman, hunter and fisherman, but he wept easily, and I imagine him with reddening, watering eyes as he stood on the platform and watched the train, a dozen passenger cars powered by an electric engine, pull out of the station.

A hundred and fifty miles to the west, at Harrisburg, Pennsylvania, a steam locomotive replaced the electric one and chugged toward the Allegheny Mountains. It passed Pittsburgh around nightfall. I wonder if, just west of Altoona, as she did with me on later trips, my mother had looked out the window as the train maneuvered the Horseshoe Curve so she could see the engine seemingly going in the opposite direction.

At Chicago, mother and child changed to one of those long and sleek transcontinental passenger trains. Also, a physician arrived to see my sister.

At some point after dark on the second day, during the 1,800-mile stretch between Chicago and Phoenix, the train slowed, then stopped. Passengers peered through the windows and, puzzled, saw that they were at some desolate spot on the Great Plains. The conductor led a physician down the aisle to my mother's seat so he could examine my sister. He wore a dark coat and carried a doctor's bag. He told my mother that he had driven an hour in order to meet the train at a crossing that was many miles from the nearest town.

The train eventually reached Phoenix where someone was waiting for the travelers. He took them to a house in a place called Tempe. In the morning, Mom took Dorothy to see the doctor.

Meanwhile, back in New Jersey, my brother Don and I were living with a family on the next block. They had three children about our age, and we stayed there for the duration of our mother's absence. I remember that Mom sent us a series of letters. Each letter contained pieces of a cardboard jigsaw puzzle, which was a map of the United States. When we put all the pieces together, we could see where Arizona was.

I don't know how long we stayed with these people. Nor do I remember exactly how long Mom was away. I have this vague notion that she returned a few days before Christmas. I do know that she came home alone. Dorothy had died during treatment in Arizona.

Memories of that sad Christmas faded away long ago, but I vividly recall Mom's story of that desperate trip and of the Salvation Army's generosity and kindnesses to a sick child and her family. Mom told and retold the tale so many times that over the years it became a family legend.

Today, at age 74, I barely remember my sister. Indeed, I can identify only one specific memory of her. There are, of course, family snapshots of Dad and Mom with the twins, so I know what my sister looked like.

I tend to think of Dorothy at Christmas, sometimes without meaning to. The other night, for example, I was taking an indoor walk at the mall when I turned the corner and happened upon a woman in a dark uniform ringing a bell and standing alongside a red kettle. All this story came rushing back, and there I was, smiling and cheerfully making small talk as I fished all the change out of my pocket and put it in the red kettle.

Some debts can't ever be repaid.

The night the opposition came in disguise

THE JANITOR I remember best from elementary school was a smiling, balding, middle-aged man with a big nose. I think he had a salt-and-pepper mustache. More than sixty years have passed since these events took place, and I'm not so sure about the mustache, but he had the kind of face that could have worn one. Everybody – by that I mean, all us kids – liked the man. He always had a funny story for us, and I picture him coming down the hall pushing a wide dry mop that was lined with dirty gray fringe. As always, he was wearing a gray shirt with a sewn-on cloth badge that said "Rocky" just below the right shoulder. We'd crowd around him in the hallway and stand in front of his dry mop until he told us a riddle or a joke. Then we'd laugh and move out of his way, and he'd go happily down the hall.

One summer – I think it was the summer before I entered 7th grade, which would have been 1954 – some of the grownups in our town (Somerville, N.J.) decided to raise money to build a swimming pool for the big kids. A high school girl – a tall, articulate teenager with brown hair and dark bushy eyebrows – had sparked the project. She had come to a human relations group to which my parents belonged and said there was nothing in town for the high school kids to do in the summer. Impressed by the girl's lament, the group decided to push for the construction of a swimming pool deep enough to attract teenagers.

As the swimming pool committee organized, Rocky the janitor became a co-chairman. My mother, Virginia E. Moore, was appointed as the other co-chair. The committee launched a series of bake sales and other money-raising activities, and donations and pledges started coming in. I remember that committee members wanted to locate the pool in a large and popular park situated along aptly named Park Avenue. The borough had a highly organized and well-attended recreational program at this park every summer.

The park contained plenty of space for such a pool. Years earlier, the town had developed parkland out of the floodplain along Peters Brook, a stream that coursed throughout the community. In a few neighborhoods, the borough had used the parkland to build playgrounds with swings, seesaws and sliding boards. A privileged few of these playgrounds even had swimming pools, but the largest of these were only three and a half feet deep. These pools provided excellent – and free – swimming for the little kids, but the big kids – those in junior and senior high – sneered at the notion of swimming with the tykes.

The pool committee had had unofficial talks with borough officials who had indicated they would be receptive to the idea of building a larger, deeper swimming pool along Park Avenue, which was all of one block long. A look at a map showing the boundaries of the town indicates that the probable site was more or less centrally located.

It seemed to me that nearly all the little kids in town came to the Park Avenue pool. Clad in bathing suits and sneakers, we'd walk or ride our bikes. Mr. Lepp, a teacher at Somerville Junior High School, ran this program every summer. I remember him as a burly man with a friendly smile and a full head of black hair. On duty at the park, Mr. Lepp usually wore khaki trousers and a white t-shirt with a whistle on a lanyard around his neck. The sharp blasts of the whistle was the signal for everybody to get out of the pool. He'd have a hundred or more dripping-wet kids line up at one end of the park, and then we'd march across the grass in our bare feet, stooping to pick up every candy bar wrapper and Popsicle stick that we encountered.

Mr. Lepp's park had become Somerville's recreational hub, at least for the kids. It was easy for my 12-year-old mind to accept the logic of the grownups, including my mother, who wanted to build a swimming pool for teenagers there. After all, I was getting bigger, and the pool that had seemed so deep to me when I was six was becoming shallower with each succeeding summer. It would be nice to become a teenager and swim in a deep pool with a diving board at my favorite park.

At the supper table, Mom kept our family apprised of the pool committee's progress. I was only a kid, so kindly cut me some slack if I'm vague on details. I remember that someone had prepared an estimate of the costs, and as the pledges approached the crucial number, the co-chairmen called a public meeting to give the proposal a thorough airing. It was a warm night in early summer. The meeting took place at a community center across Park Avenue from Mr. Lepp's park.

I was impressed that so many people turned out. I sat about half way back, close enough to hear and see what my mother and the other committee members might say and far enough back to get a good sense of the crowd. The evening was warm, and the place was packed. Aside from attending church on Easter Sunday, I don't think I had ever sat in a hall with so many grownups and so few children.

Somebody up front – my mother? – reported on the progress of the fund drive, announcing that as of tonight cash donations plus the latest pledges exceeded the goal. This good news generated an enthusiastic round of applause. Someone up front said that the committee now had the commitments needed to begin serious negotiations to win the borough's approval to build the pool, most likely in the vicinity of but not necessarily adjacent to the pool for the younger kids.

Suddenly several rows in front of me a man wearing a white shirt stood up. He lived in my neighborhood and his children went to my school. The chair recognized him The audience quieted, and he began to speak, starting off with something congratulatory to the committee. Then he said, "But we don't have enough money for two pools."

There was a gasp, and I heard somebody up front – was it my mother? – say, "Two pools? We only intend to build one pool."

The man replied, "But we need two pools. It's too far for the kids on the west end to walk all the way to a swimming pool down here."

Here and there, other people joined in. "That's right," a man said. "Two pools," a woman said.

The man's remark had created such a stir that the meeting stalled. More than a few people had expressed agreement. I saw members of the committee form a huddle, and then my mother announced that the meeting was over. It had lasted all of fifteen minutes. Twenty at the most.

The committee, my mother announced, needed to hold an executive meeting to consider this surprise development, and would do so within the hour at another location.

The committee headed to my house some six blocks away. Outside, there was plenty of daylight left. I remember racing home on my bike, pedaling furiously to reach the house ahead of the committee. I held the screen door open as Rocky, my mother and the other committee members came up the front steps.

A short, trim woman with dark hair, my mother, then in her late 30s, had grown up in Pittsburgh, Pennsylvania. An idealist by nature, she had both a strong altruistic and entrepreneurial approach to life. She possessed a voice that, when she got riled, could pierce.

As their meeting began, I wanted to sit in, but my mother explained that only members of the pool committee could attend. Ejected from the living room in my own home, I did the next best thing. My father had taken down the storm sash and put up the screens. My mother had opened the windows to provide ventilation, and I stood under the open windows and listened. I don't believe anybody ever realized I was there, so I overheard the entire proceeding.

Inside, the meeting heated up. My mother and several other members said they were perplexed that some people felt a need for two pools. The town was small, and the pool would be centrally located. Teenagers would be able to walk or to ride their bikes to it from all over town.

It didn't take much prodding for some of the other members to disclose the reason. The town's residential areas were racially segregated, and not quite a mile to the west – but still within reasonable walking distance – was a neighborhood inhabited mainly by black people. Should a second pool be built, it would likely go there.

As the discussion proceeded, I heard Rocky blurt out, "A lot of people don't want their kids swimming with niggers."

My mother's retort came loud, angry and sharp: "Don't use that word in my house!"

As crude as his remark had been, Rocky had exposed the reef on which the pool committee wrecked. The effort to build the pool died right there.

"Either we build one pool or we don't build any pool," my mother said.

In the end, the segregationists won out, preferring no pool to one pool for everybody regardless of race.

Acknowledging defeat, the committee began the sad task of refunding all the cash contributions and voiding all the pledges.

Then it disbanded.

I remember my mother telling me years later that a middle-age black man she knew had told her: "I have lived in this town all of my life, and I never realized that I was a second-class citizen until that night at the community center."

A boy's memories of Girl Scout camp

IT MUST HAVE BEEN April 1955. I was twelve. My mother's grand plan was to develop a Girl Scout camp in a wooded glen on New Jersey's Sourland Mountain, not far from the village of Neshanic. It lay some 40 miles due west of a better known place, an island called Manhattan.

My father was her most enthusiastic supporter, and, on sunny Sunday afternoons, her chief worker. After Sunday dinner we piled our gear into our '48 Hudson, a huge gray sedan with lots of room in the trunk. In went an axe, a crowbar, a large saw for pruning tree limbs, work gloves, sheathed hatchets for the use of my younger brother and me, a first-aid kit with plenty of Band-Aids, a thermos of coffee for the grownups, a jug of hot cocoa for the kids, and a sack of sandwiches for a cold supper. Unless a storm blew up, we would work in the woods until shortly before sunset.

We only lived fifteen miles from the mountain, but it always took forever for the Hudson to travel that far. But finally, we left the paved road and turned down a long gravel lane, stopping where a bridge had once crossed a brook. The bridge had tumbled down long ago, and we parked near its ruins. We unloaded our gear and crossed the brook on stepping stones and walked up the path that led to the camp.

It wasn't a camp yet – just a woods, a garage and an old house, long vacant, whose yard was overgrown with a thicket of saplings, mostly ailanthus trees.

Mom and Dad had taught us that this tree had a nickname – tree of heaven. But Donald and I had given them a name of our own. We had been assigned to chop them down, and we called them "stink trees" because they exuded a rank odor when we cut into the bark.

I remember this day vividly. The sky was deep blue and clear of clouds, but the air was cool, almost chilly, and we had to wear jackets. It was early spring. Most of the bushes and underbrush had grown new leaves, but the leaves were just sprouting on the trees, especially the tallest ones.

Wildflowers had bloomed here and there, and the mountain breeze carried the aroma of spring. Within minutes my brother and I were deep in the thicket of ailanthus trees, hacking and chopping, and laughing at how foul they smelled. They were weeds, and our task was to cut them all down. We trimmed some of the smaller shoots to the size of spears, and hurled them at invisible enemies in the bush.

Some other families had turned out for the work party, and Mom and another woman stood in front of the door to the house, pulling weeds and talking. Dad was hard at work a short way from the old garage, intent on removing an old tree. Obviously dead for years, it had toppled over, snapping the trunk about seven or eight feet above the ground. All that remained was the huge thick trunk, bare of bark, still upright. My father was easily six feet tall, and the top of the tree extended a full foot above his head.

Dad yelled over that the trunk was severely rotted, and would be easy to pull down. I remember watching as he reached high up and grabbed a large branch close to the top of the trunk. He was wearing work gloves and a heavy red-and-black flannel shirt. He tugged hard, and the branch ripped free. He tossed the branch aside and grabbed again at the trunk, this time grasping at a large section of the outer bark. I turned back to the smelly task of ridding the yard of the Tree of Heaven.

Minutes later a commotion erupted at the old tree. My father was shouting, "Hey, everybody!" He was waving his arm, and a large raccoon held fast to his sleeve. It hissed and snarled and bit at the work glove that protected his hand.

My brother and I dropped our hatchets and ran over. Other people came over, too.

"Not too close," Dad cautioned. He was grinning, really enjoying the excitement. He moved his arm so that we could all get a good look at the raccoon. I noted that he kept the animal as far away from his face as he could.

"The tree is hollow," Dad said. "When I pulled part of the side loose, she came out with it. I think she has a nest inside."

The raccoon remained fastened to his arm, and after a long minute, Dad walked over to the bushes behind the stump and carefully lowered his arm. When the raccoon was about three feet from the ground, she jumped free and raced into the bushes. We never saw her again.

Dad walked over to the stump, and looked into to the hollow. "She has pups in there," he said.

I was closest and he motioned for me to come over. The hole was a good foot over my head and he hoisted me up for a quick look. I remember seeing four or five tiny animals, all with their eyes closed. It was a fascinating sight. Then he held my brother and the other children so they could all see. After that, he gave the grownups a chance.

When everybody had gotten a look, he explained that we all had to go to another part of the camp for the rest of the afternoon. That would give the raccoon the privacy she needed to move her babies to a new home. So we walked to another work area several hundred yards away. The afternoon passed quickly, but without any new adventures. Soon it was nearly sunset, and we loaded our equipment into the car.

Before we drove away, we went up to the old hollow tree to see if the babies were still there. Dad looked inside first, just in case the mother raccoon was inside. But she wasn't. He held Donald and me up for a peek. With considerable wonder, we saw that the pups were gone.

My brother and I learned a lesson about life in the wild that afternoon. I have never forgotten the fury with which the mother raccoon attacked an invader many times her size in order to protect her helpless blind babies.

Dad died not many years after that, but the understanding and respect he demonstrated for wild animals that afternoon has stayed with me for nearly 70 years. In my mind's eye, I still see him – a hardy man in a red-and-black checked shirt, holding his arm high up to show us the raging raccoon. He grins as she snarls.

It is one of my most cherished memories.

How Mom invented the inflatable swimming pool

BACK IN THE early 1950s, we lived in a residential neighborhood in a small New Jersey town. My father worked at a nearby plastics factory that made a material we all called Vinylite.

The Vinylite I knew came in one color – army surplus green. The material was similar to the heavy duty trash bags available in stores today. You know it as vinyl.

Dad bought it in long, thin sheets at the factory's outlet store. His interest in Vinylite was strictly practical. When vacation time rolled around, we invariably packed our canvas tent in the car and headed to a distant state park for two weeks of camping. We used Vinylite for a table cloth, a tarpaulin over the campsite's picnic table, and a liner for the floor of the tent.

One year – I was nine or ten – summer became unbearably humid and hot. Nobody in our neighborhood had air conditioners. A man in the next block dug a hole in his backyard, then used concrete to make a small swimming pool for his children. My brother and I pleaded with Dad to build a pool in our backyard, but he said no, repeatedly and emphatically.

Mom, always an imaginative thinker, saw the Vinylite as a readily available resource to help us cool off. A stay-at-home mother (as most mothers were in 1951), she assembled her tools – a yardstick, marker, scissors, a cotton towel, ironing board and iron, and vacuum cleaner.

"We're making a swimming pool," Mom told us.

If they existed at all, inflatable pools were very rare. Certainly, we had never seen one, and we had no idea what she was talking about.

Nevertheless, my brother and I helped her as she unrolled a large section of Vinylite over the living room rug, measured and marked the section she wanted, then used her scissors to cut out a circle about four feet across.

Then she marked and cut a long rectangle. "This will form the sides," she said.

After 60-plus years my memory's become a little hazy on what happened next, but at some point, she used the iron and ironing board to fuse the long rectangular piece into a circular tube. She then fused the bottom of the tube onto the edges of the circular piece.

As per Mom's direction, my brother and I took the hose off the suction end of the vacuum cleaner and inserted it in the exhaust end. We then placed the other end into a special hole in the side of our strange contraption. We turned the vacuum cleaner on, and the sides of the swimming pool filled with air.

We carefully transported the inflated device out to the backyard, found a smooth place, and gently laid it down on the grass. Then we used the garden hose to aim a gentle stream of water into the pool.

"Will it leak?" we wanted to know.

We were amazed when the water remained in the pool. We were delighted when Mom told us to change into our bathing suits and take a dip.

As Don and I cooled off, Mom used a Brownie camera to take some snapshots of us and her inflatable pool.

As summer ended, a friend of my father's came to visit. He was an engineer in the plastics factory. He took his notebook out of his shirt pocket and started taking notes as Mom told him about her

Vinylite swimming pool. He asked a variety of questions, and they talked for a long time. I remember clearly that she went upstairs and came down with the photos she had taken. If memory's correct, she gave him several photos to take with him.

At any rate, within a year or two, retail stores began to sell inflatable wading pools made of red or blue plastic. They became quite popular, and many families with small children bought them.

But we didn't. We had moved on. It had occurred to Mom that she could use sturdy metal fencing – about 18 inches high – and construct a pool about four feet wide and eight or nine feet long, capable of holding at least a foot of water.

Somewhere there are photos of Don and me wearing goggles and holding toy boats as we sat in the pool. He and I may be the only people who know this story. Now you do, too.

Young Pa. man sought fortune in Texas, found destiny instead

IN DECEMBER 1835, David Cummings of Lewistown left Pennsylvania, heading for Texas to seek his fortune. Little did he know that he would soon meet his destiny in an old Spanish mission called The Alamo.

A surveyor, the 26-year-old Cummings took his surveying instruments, a small shipment of rifles and a letter of introduction to General Sam Houston. Texas was then part of Mexico, and Houston, an old friend of Cummings' father, was leading a rebellion against Mexican rule.

In a January 20 letter to his father, Cummings reported that he had arrived in the East Texas town of Gonzales. He said that he wanted "to connect myself with a company of rangers on the frontiers to keep off the Indians, But it is most probable I will go on to San Antonio de Bexar and there remain until I can suitably connect myself with the army or until an occasion may require my services."

San Antonio is about 75 miles west of Gonzales.

Texas had begun giving tracts of undeveloped land to newly arrived immigrants from the United States. Not only did Cummings want to acquire land for himself, but he also saw the distribution of land as a business opportunity. "I will most likely be engaged in surveying of public lands," Cummings said in a second letter to his father, this one written at San Antonio on February 14.

Shortly after writing this letter, Cummings left The Alamo, if only temporarily.

The Alamo mission, which Texas revolutionaries had fortified in late 1835 and early 1836, was located at San Antonio de Bexar. It occupied a strategic spot along a key road leading from Mexico to settlements in the Texas interior. If Mexican soldiers showed up to suppress the Texas revolution, The Alamo's garrison had orders to send out riders to spread the alarm inland.

Led by General Antonio López de Santa Anna, the Mexican army arrived at The Alamo on Tuesday, February 23, and the next day began firing cannons at the mission.

On the night of Wednesday, February 24, Col. William Travis sent a rider with an urgent message to Gonzales: "Come to our aid with all dispatch . . ."

The men in Gonzales were already organizing a company of rangers when the messenger, Capt. Albert Martin, arrived. Martin passed Travis' note along to another rider, but first he scribbled on the back of the note: "We were very short of ammunition when I left. Hurry on all the men you can get in haste."

The second courier then rode off to San Felipe, about 90 miles farther east.

On Saturday, February 27, the Gonzales rangers departed for The Alamo. "Loaded with rifles, blankets and food, 25 men rode out of town," reported author Stephen L. Moore in a 2007 book, *Savage Frontier: Rangers, Riflemen, and Indian Wars in Texas.*

On Sunday, February 28, the rangers reached a ford on the Cibolo River, not far from San Antonio. "They stopped long enough to look for extra recruits," Moore wrote. "They found some, including David Cummings, who had previously been in The Alamo garrison."

On Monday, February 29, "the men rested . . . and prepared to make an evening dash into Bexar," Moore said. "The rangers crossed the river at sunset and moved west toward The Alamo."

The 32 men of the Gonzales Mounted Ranger Company "cautiously skirted Mexican soldiers during the bitterly cold night until arriving within sight of The Alamo. They rushed into the old fortress at 3 a.m.," Moore wrote.

Six days later – on Sunday, March 6 – Mexican soldiers stormed the mission and killed all 189 defenders, the Lewistown surveyor among them.

As his men rushed The Alamo, little did the 42-year-old Santa Anna know that 33 years later, he would be exiled from Mexico and would travel to Staten Island, New York. There he met an inventor, Thomas Adams, who purchased a large quantity of chicle from him. Chicle is made from the sticky sap of a Central American tree, the sapodilla. Adams used it in unsuccessful attempts to develop a substitute for rubber, according to the 1996 edition of *The Encyclopedia of New York City*.

The article also quoted a 1944 speech that Horatio Adams, Thomas' grandson, made at a function of the American Chicle Co. Then in his 90s, Horatio told the chewing gum manufacturers that one night his grandfather was in the corner drug store when a child came in and bought some chewing gum for a penny. Chewing gum sold by retailers in those days often consisted of sweetened and flavored paraffin. The girl's purchase prompted Adams to think of the large quantity of chicle that he had purchased from Santa Anna and was now ready to throw away.

"When he asked the man if he would be willing to try an entirely different kind of gum, the druggist agreed," Horatio said. "When Mr. Thomas Adams arrived home that night, he spoke to his son, Tom Jr., my father, about his idea. Junior was very much impressed, and suggested that they make up a few boxes of chicle chewing gum and give it a name and a label."

The Adamses came up with C*hiclets*, and the rest, as they say, was history.

As a boy in the early 1950s, I liked to take short cuts as I walked to school. I lived in Somerville, N.J., about 25 miles west of Staten Island.

One of my favorite routes crossed the property of a very old man we all said was a millionaire. He and his very elderly wife lived in a Victorian mansion built of dark stone. There was a cobblestone drive that led from the street to the mansion's porch. I vividly recall seeing the old man get into an ancient automobile while an elderly chauffeur held the rear door open.

When not in use, the car was kept in the carriage house behind the mansion. A retaining wall separated a large garden from the driveway to the carriage house.

I remember pushing myself up and over the retaining wall, then running as fast as I could toward the mansion's porch. Several other boys were running with me. Our goal was to touch the porch, then race off although we all knew that the property owner, a frail old man, was probably waiting to chase us away.

Sometimes the old man stood just inside the porch door, watching for us at the window. Other times he walked onto the porch as we started our charge. When that happened, few of us had nerve enough to approach the porch. We'd abruptly change course, and head for the street.

Either way, we'd cross the street, and then we'd turn to face him, forming a kind of chorus line. In sing-song voices we'd chant at the top of our lungs: "Chiclets! Chiclets! Yeah. Yeah. Chiclets!" Then we'd race off to school.

As a child, I never understood what the chant meant.

Little did I know that the father and grandfather of this ancient man had invented chewing gum and once had business dealings with the infamous Santa Anna.

Half a century passed before I learned that when Horatio Adams died at 102 in 1956, his obituary ran in newspapers and magazines across the country. Even *Time* magazine devoted 42 words to his passing.

Editor's note: Additional sources for this article included The Handbook of Texas Online, a project of the Texas State Historical Association; "Forever Texas: Texas, The Way Those Who Lived It Wrote It," edited by Mike Blakely and Mary Elizabeth Goldman; and "Tejanos in the 1835 Texas Revolution" by L. Lloyd MacDonald.

1953 issue of Playboy causes crisis for the paperboy

THE FIRST ISSUE of Playboy magazine came out in December 1953. I picked up a copy in my hometown of Somerville, N.J., one wintry afternoon in 1954. No, I didn't buy it.

I was 11 years old and a student in the 5th grade. As I delivered newspapers along my route one day, I saw a magazine laying on the grass between the sidewalk and the curb. The cover had a picture of a blond lady I didn't recognize. Ever curious, I stopped, picked it up, and paged through it.

The photographs amazed me. Never had I seen such sights. One glance, and I knew that I'd be in big trouble if I got caught with it. At the very least, my parents would confiscate it.

So I stuffed the magazine in my newspaper bag and continued delivering my papers. I'd have plenty of time to examine the pictures later when I had some privacy and some leisure.

As I neared home, I had to decide: should I hide the magazine, which was in nearly new condition, in the hole in a big tree in the woods near my house, or should I stash it in the crawl space in the top of our garage?

The hole in the tree would be dry, but other kids occasionally kept stuff in there, and I didn't want to put it where somebody else might swipe it. My father sometimes ventured into the top of the garage to retrieve something he had stored, but that wasn't likely tonight since it would be dark by the time he got home from work.

I calculated that there was greater risk of some kid's taking it from the tree than of my father's finding it in the garage, so I hid the *Playboy* in the garage, at least for the night. I had already decided that tomorrow I'd take it to school and show the other boys at lunchtime.

As I left for school in the morning, I doubt that I told my mom I had to stop in the garage, but I did stop there. Stealthily, I slipped the magazine inside my bulky woolen coat, and dashed off to school.

The day was cold but sunny – perfect weather for showing off the magazine during our 30-minute recess on the playground after lunch.

The boys had a favorite place to congregate – off to the side of the playground, against a brick wall that was part of a school building. Often five or six of us would flip baseball cards against the wall. Whoever owned the card that got closest to the wall won all of the other cards.

But today my magazine became the chief attraction, and an extra-large group of boys crowded in to see. The photos of some topless French dancers caused quite a stir. I remember some nosy girls trying to elbow their way into the group, but the boys at the edge of the crowd rebuffed them.

"Dirty pictures," I heard a girl shout. "They're looking at dirty pictures."

"Let's go get the teacher," another girl said loudly.

The teacher on playground duty that day was Miss Benson, an older woman with gray hair. We called her "Bulldog Benson." She wore a dark cloth coat that came down well below her knees. Despite the crowd around me, I saw her walking slowly across the far end of the playground. I watched the girls run to her, and presently she started walking in our direction. It seemed that she was moving extra quickly. A growing number of girls accompanied her.

As it happened, the other boys and I were standing alongside a large one-story wooden shed in which the janitors stored trash from the classrooms. The shed had a flat roof.

As the teacher closed in, I just stood there like a deer in the headlights, but the boy standing on my immediate left suddenly grabbed the magazine out of my hands. He hurled it with terrific speed and force up over the crowd and way back onto the roof of the storage shed.

I can still hear the sound of *Playboy* whooshing through the air as it hurtled out of my sight.

The teacher stopped in her tracks. The crowd of boys dispersed. None of us ever suffered any consequences. As for the *Playboy*, I never saw it again. To this day, I don't know if any of the janitors got out a ladder and climbed to the roof to retrieve it.

I was much too young to sense that a small fortune had literally slipped through my fingers. According to a posting on greatestcollectibles.com, in 2013 an original *Playboy* from December 1953 sold for $4,550 on eBay.

The blonde on the cover, whom I didn't recognize in 1954, turned out to be Marilyn Monroe.

A family's history can sometimes harbor a real stinker

MY FATHER – Leon H. Moore Jr. – had a way with skunks. So did his younger brother, Willis.

Long ago, as Dad drove us past the elementary school he had attended in Lambertville, N. J., he pointed to the window of a second-floor classroom. He had been a pupil in that classroom. He said that one winter he decided he wanted a day off. He couldn't just play hooky because he had done that – and been caught – too many times. So he and his brother decided to close the school for a day.

They went out to the woods with a large cloth sack and caught a skunk. When it got dark, they took the skunk to the school building and held it up to a vent in the heating system. Irritated, the skunk sprayed.

When the principal and janitor arrived in the morning, they canceled school until the aroma cleared.

Thus Dad and Uncle Willis had the day off. So did everybody else, but the Moore boys got in trouble anyway. They smelled more like skunk than anybody else.

Dad must have been 11 or 12 when this happened, so that places the year as 1916 or 1917, although it could have been as early as 1915, when he was ten.

As adults, Dad and Uncle Willis continued to play with skunks.

I remembered visiting Uncle Willis and Aunt Jewel in Trenton, N.J., in the 1950s. They had a pet skunk, an adolescent, and Willis said he intended to have the animal descented. They also had a pet cat. One day, the cat picked a fight with the skunk before Willis had it fixed. Both animals were in the house, and the cat, upset that he had been sprayed, jumped up on Aunt Jewel for comfort.

As my uncle told us later, cat and wife got banished to the garage while Willis went to the store for huge quantities of tomato juice, then a popular antidote for skunk spray.

I don't remember whatever happened to the skunk.

My parents met in Pittsburgh during the 1936 Flood. Mom worked at the cigarette/candy counter of a shop in the first floor of a downtown office building, and Dad was an electrician working for Western Union. He had been sent to Pittsburgh as part of the flood recovery effort.

Mom was a city girl, but they moved to the New Jersey countryside after they got married and lived in a bungalow along a gravel road. For a while they raised chickens and goats.

One day, Dad placed a large burlap sack over one end of a metal culvert that ran under the road near their house. He asked Mom to come hold the sack, explaining that there was a rabbit hiding in the culvert. If she kept the sack in place, he'd cross the road and drive the rabbit into the bag.

She did as directed, and within a minute or two, the critter ran into the bag.

"Look, Leon," she shouted. "The rabbit's in the sack."

He hollered back: "Whatever you do, Ginny, don't drop the bag! It's not a rabbit. It's a skunk!"

The marriage somehow survived the prank, and the skunk got away.

This happened before I came along. Dad liked to tell the story, and Mom always laughed.

Dad's last summer was in 1959. He took Mom, little brother Don and me camping in a canvas tent for a week in June at Shawnee State Park along Route 30 in south-central Pennsylvania. In those days, most campers used canvas tents. RVs and camper trailers hadn't yet become popular.

Don and I had gone down to the lake after supper. It was dusk as we walked back to our campsite. I remember hearing a hubbub and seeing a lot of campers, grownups as well as children, standing in a ring in the midst of the tents.

I remember one voice say distinctly: "Look at the crazy man petting the skunk!"

The man was our dad, and he was indeed petting the skunk on the nose. What an unforgettable sight! The campers were both fascinated and horrified. If the skunk sprayed, the campground could well become uninhabitable, at least for a few days.

Suddenly the skunk raised its tail, causing an audible stir in the crowd, but Dad quickly and confidently used his hand to push the tail back down. No spraying occurred.

We saw that ever so slowly, he was maneuvering the skunk to the woods at the edge of the camping area.

When they got the trees, the skunk scampered into the forest, and the campers breathed a great sigh of relief.

In a profound way, this was Dad's finest hour. I remember him standing there, smiling happily as the crowd dispersed. He had put on a grand performance.

Ray & I were just going to a march, not marching into history

HISTORY HAPPENS. Once in a rare while, you might be in it, but most of the time you aren't.

As I ate lunch one day recently, I was reading a *Time* magazine article about Martin Luther King's great March on Washington on August 28, 1963. The photographs of the crowd caught my attention, because I was in there somewhere. I looked closely for pictures of myself and my friend Ray. There was a photo of Marlon Brando, Harry Belafonte and Charlton Heston getting off the plane from Hollywood, but no pictures of us, which didn't surprise me at all.

Ray and I were in our early 20s. Except for a few of his friends, nobody was expecting us. We had no thought that we were doing anything historic. We were just going to a march. I didn't even take my camera.

I grew up in New Jersey during the 1950s. My predominantly white town had a few policemen, school teachers and physicians who were black. Many whites I knew used the N-word frequently, even habitually. Even at church, I often heard derogatory remarks about blacks.

I lived close enough to New York City for my AM radio to get clear reception of a radio station that broadcast Jocko and his all-night Rocket Ship Show. He'd count down as his program began:

"Three. Two. One. Blast off!" Then the rhythm and blues would start. Like Jocko, the musicians were black. I loved the music.

I remember driving across the American South during the summer of 1960, with stops in New Orleans; Jackson, Mississippi; and Roanoke, Virginia. The racial discrimination I saw appalled me. The public restaurants and restrooms were segregated. So were the hotels we stayed in.

One day we had a picnic in a public park in Jackson. When I got thirsty, I went to the drinking fountain for a drink and saw that each fountain had two sides. Black people stood in a line to drink from the "colored" spout, and whites lined up to drink from the one marked "white." I felt quite uncomfortable as I got in the white line.

My memory of segregated Jackson was still fresh when in 1961 Freedom Riders took buses into the South and challenged the racial segregation practices at interstate public transportation facilities. When they reached Jackson, hundreds were arrested and hauled off to jail.

I admired the Freedom Riders' courage, and abhorred the violent reception Southern whites gave them.

Fast forward to August 1963. Congress was considering civil rights legislation, and a call went out for a massive march on Washington. Ray and I decided to go, and we drove from New Jersey to DC in his VW bug, a convertible. We stayed with friends of his in DC, got up early and walked to the Washington Monument, then marched with a quarter million other people to the Lincoln Memorial.

I had participated in occasional demonstrations previously, but they had been tiny. I remember thinking that we were a human sea. Even so, I was startled later when I saw aerial photos of all the people. I have read that as many as an estimated 300,000 marchers participated and that at least 75 percent of them were black. That seems about right.

There had been well-publicized fears that the demonstration would turn violent, but everybody I met seemed friendly, even happy.

The day was hot, and the sun was bright. Ray and I stood somewhere between the Lincoln Memorial and the Reflecting Pool, close enough to plainly see the faces of the speakers. There were all sorts of celebrities: actors and singers. Joan Baez sang "We Shall Overcome." Peter, Paul and Mary sang their signature song, "If I Had a Hammer." Bob Dylan also performed.

In my mind, I can see civil rights activists standing on the platform and delivering serious speeches, but these particular memories grew dim long ago. Dr. King's great "I-Have-a-Dream-Speech" was surely moving, but I have seen it on television so many times that electronic images have replaced my own memory of it.

One memory remains clear: dancing and singing, a line of 20 or 25 young blacks – people my own age – come down the street. They move rhythmically and sing a spirited gospel song that is new to me: "This little light of mine ... let it shine."

In terms of U.S. history, the march accomplished two things:

1. It angered many white people across the country, North and South. Back home in New Jersey, many of my friends and relatives were annoyed when I told them I had taken part.

2. It prompted Congress to pass the Civil Rights Act of 1964 and the Voting Rights Act of 1965.

I regard the march as an exemplary expression of the First Amendment, especially "the right of the people peaceably to assemble, and to petition the government for a redress of grievances."

Looking back, I see that I have long sought to promote the belief "that all men are created equal." This was an essential element in King's speech. He wanted Thomas Jefferson's radical notion of 1776 broadened to include "black men as well as white men." To a limited extent, this has happened.

As I write this, I find myself singing, "This little light of mine. Let it shine. Let it shine."

One (mad)man's 1965 plan to head off global thermonuclear war

DURING THE 1960s, many Americans believed that the threat of world-wide nuclear war was very real. I know I did.

After all, the USSR had hundreds of nuclear missiles aimed at the U.S., and we had hundreds of nuclear missiles aimed at them. In school we had frequent nuclear disaster drills: our teachers took us out into the hall, away from the widows, and made us stand facing the wall. They made us put our hands across the back of our necks, and stand there until we heard the all clear signal.

The Cuban Missile Crisis of 1962 remained fresh in everyone's mind. There was even a 1964 movie, a comedy, titled, *Dr. Strangelove or: How I Learned to Stop Worrying and Love the Bomb.*

Many of us believed that creating global peace was the most important thing in the world, but I only ever met one person who appeared truly and deeply committed to bringing it about.

In January 1965, I was living in Bethlehem, Pennsylvania, and looking for work. A friend and I had spent Monday going over the classified ads in the Sunday newspaper, and calling employers whose ads appealed to us. We made several appointments, then used my manual typewriter to write our resumes.

On Tuesday, we took the bus to Allentown. She had an 11 a.m. interview with someone looking for an executive secretary, and I had a 1:30 appointment at the same address because someone there also wanted an executive assistant. As we got off the bus, we decided to meet at 4 o'clock in a restaurant on Hamilton Street, the main thoroughfare.

I remember walking into a stiff wind as I headed toward the 900 block of Linden Street at a few minutes early for my 1:30. I opened a wrought iron gate and walked the short distance to the steps of a Victorian-era brick residence. I climbed the steps, rang the doorbell and was quickly greeted by a white-haired man with a pleasant face and voice.

A thin man, he wore a white shirt, dark tie and a brown suit. His neatly trimmed white beard was shaped to a point – a Van Dyke.

He introduced himself. I long ago forgot his first name, but his surname was Pennsylvania German and began with a B – something like Bergstresser, Burkholder or Barnhardt.

He led me into the front room, which had dark wallpaper and dark woodwork. There were two wooden chairs in front of his wooden desk, on top of which were a telephone and a pad of yellow notepaper. He sat behind the desk and motioned for me to sit on one of the wooden chairs.

As I handed him my one-page resume, he began to explain that he was organizing an initiative for world peace. He planned to invite all of the world leaders to a summit meeting at the Allentown Fairgrounds in August. He needed a staff of three: an executive secretary, an executive assistant, and an advance man.

He struck me as being very earnest, very sincere, but I was becoming skeptical.

The advance man, he explained, would travel around the world and persuade the world leaders to come to Allentown and take part in the conference.

The executive assistant would work out of the Linden Street office and coordinate travel arrangements for the world leaders. The secretary would take dictation, type letters and handle telephone calls.

"This morning," he said, "I interviewed a nice young woman for the secretary's position."

The remark made me uncomfortable, and I began to worry about my friend. Also, I was beginning to think the old man was mad.

The longer he talked, the more he reminded me of a character in "The Lesson," a play by the absurdist playwright Eugène Ionesco that we had performed in college. With a subdued flippancy, I began to respond to his questions and comments by saying, "Yes, professor," or "No, professor," just like the student in the play.

My responses pleased him. He smiled and became much more animated.

At one point, the professor looked at me sternly, and told me flat out that I lacked the qualities and credentials he required for the position of executive assistant.

Then he smiled and said, "I am hiring you as my advance man."

He explained that he would first send me to the A countries – Albania, Angola, Argentina. Then I would visit all the B countries – Belgium, Burma, Brazil. After that I'd move on to the C countries – Canada, Columbia, Cambodia. And so on.

"You start on Monday morning," the old man said. "Be here at 9 o'clock sharp. Bring your suitcase."

We shook hands, and I left.

Later that afternoon, I felt relieved when my friend joined me for coffee at the Hamilton Street eatery. She had been a psychology major, and as we compared notes, we quickly agreed that Professor B. was mad.

I didn't call or write to decline the position of advance man. I just didn't show up on Monday morning. Neither did my friend, whom he had hired as the executive secretary.

I never saw the old man again. As August arrived months later, I watched the newspapers closely for articles about a world peace conference in Allentown. There weren't any.

Professor B. truly believed that world peace was not only possible, but also actually achievable. Had I reported for work, could I have helped the elderly madman bring it about? Probably not.

Even so, every year as August approaches, I always feel a little guilty, especially if armed conflict is occurring anywhere in Africa, Australia, Argentina or elsewhere in the world. As I write this (on a sunny day in August 2014), I am chagrined to realize our government has just warned of a new threat from Al-Qaeda, possibly coming from Arabia.

Elderly road warrior rides in remembrance of KIAs, MIAs

WHEN I WROTE this piece during June 2016, our family's road warrior – a 70-year-old Vietnam veteran who happens to be my kid brother – was on the road again. For a septuagenarian, he was making good time.

On June 2, Don left our home in Northumberland, Pennsylvania, on his motorcycle. Two days later, he stopped for lunch at a McDonald's in Marshalltown, Iowa. I know because he posted an update on his Facebook page from Marshalltown. So he and his blue Harley-Davidson were somewhere east of Omaha. By June 5, he was in Yankton, South Dakota.

Riding solo and pushing it, Don reached his home in Tacoma, Washington, on June 8 – in time to attend his granddaughter's high school graduation.

Don had left Tacoma nearly a month earlier – on May 13 – headed for California on the first leg of his round trip transcontinental trek. In Los Angeles, he connected with hundreds of other vets, and they set out for Washington, D.C. and their annual rendezvous at the Vietnam Veterans Memorial.

This was Don's seventh Run for the Wall. Once again, his bike carried the names of American soldiers killed or missing, mainly from Vietnam, but I spotted two that I knew were from earlier wars.

Richard Vester was a 19-year-old private in the U.S. Army aboard the SS Leopoldville when a German submarine sunk the ship in the English

Channel on Christmas Eve 1944. Richard and 750 other soldiers died. His body was never recovered.

The other name I recognized was that of Richard's older brother, John.

John Vester graduated from the U.S. Military Academy at West Point in 1946. When the Korean War began, he was sent to Korea. He held the rank of captain in the army's 2nd Division Artillery when he and 600 other American soldiers were captured by the Chinese Communists in February 1951.

According to the website West-Point.org, "Official Army records indicate that John died of malnutrition as a POW on 31 May 1951." He was 29.

Neither Don nor I ever knew Richard or John, but our parents knew their parents, and the two families were friends.

I don't know for certain, but John and my Aunt Emily may have even been high school sweethearts. Emily, who died two decades ago, told me once how handsome John had looked in his uniform. She was in her late 60s then, and tears ran down her face as she talked about him.

In the early 1950s, my family often rented a cottage on Long Beach Island on the Jersey shore for a week or two. We'd spend the time fishing in the bay and getting tossed by the waves in the ocean. But one year, events in Korea clouded our sunny week at the beach. The North Koreans were releasing American POWs, and the newspapers were running long lists of the names of newly freed U.S. prisoners.

Every morning after breakfast that week, our mother walked to a nearby store and bought that day's *New York Times*. Back in the cottage, she spread the pages on the large round table and began to pore over the lists, looking for John Vester's name. Some mornings she gave me a page or two to read.

Her hopes died hard: the soldier's name wasn't ever there. However, one of the American POWs released that month had been the last U.S. soldier to see him alive. The man came home and told John's family what had happened.

To the best of my knowledge, John's remains have never been repatriated.

The names of John and Richard Vester live on if only because Brother Don carries them proudly on his Harley.

Big words, huge dictionary turned Scrabble into squabble

MY PARENTS SURVIVED the Great Depression by using their wits. By the time my brother and I came along during the 1940s, they had become incredibly frugal people.

We rarely ate in restaurants. Dad always bought a used car and did most of his own repairs. Mom made many of her own clothes and made most meals from scratch. One of the few things we ever bought new was a chest freezer.

We lived in a small town in New Jersey. At a time when our neighbors were buying brand-new television sets with tiny 12-inch screens, measured diagonally, we went to nearby farms and purchased large batches of corn, peaches, beans and other edible crops. Mom prepared them for the freezer, with token assists from my brother and me. We also bought poultry and other meats directly from the farmer.

When we finally purchased a TV, it was a second-hand set.

I don't know where Mom and Dad obtained the yellow dictionary, but I doubt they bought it new. It consisted of two thick volumes, and had hundreds if not thousands of pages, all illustrated. We consulted it whenever somebody was curious about the meaning or origin of a particular word, which was often. Each volume had a thick yellow cover.

The two volumes had a secondary use after church on Sundays when the four of us assembled for dinner, which Mom served in the dining room. My brother was too small to sit on the dining room chairs without the help of a booster seat, so he sat on one, if not both, of the yellow books.

As it does in all families, time passed and brought many changes. My brother grew and one day didn't need the dictionaries anymore. Mom became a high school Latin teacher. Dad died one Sunday morning in 1960, and I went off to college six months after that.

For many years, the thick yellow volumes were relegated to the bookcase in the living room and were rarely consulted.

Around 1970, Mom's older brother, who had lived in western Pennsylvania, came to live with her in New Jersey. Mom and Uncle Harry had always been good friends, but they had also been good-natured rivals. Blessed with strong personalities, each could be eccentric, stubborn and articulate.

Soon Uncle Harry and Mom started to play Scrabble regularly. They'd sit at the dining room table and play by the hour. Let me add here that Mom's mid-life study of Latin had expanded her vocabulary significantly.

At the Scrabble board at least, this gave her an edge over Harry – and practically everybody else she ever played.

Harry was more than a good sport. He always challenged Mom whenever she played such Latin derivatives as "ubiquitous," "omniscient" or "penultimate." To counter Harry's thrust, Mom quickly hauled out the yellow dictionary, and Uncle Harry invariably lost the challenge.

At some point, Uncle Harry must have tired of Mom's home-field advantage, because as they sat down to play one afternoon, he put a book on the table – an official Scrabble dictionary. Then he declared: "Whenever someone challenges a word, this is the dictionary we'll use to resolve the challenge. If the word's not in this book, it won't be allowed!"

In short, Harry was saying that Mom couldn't defend her words by resorting to that time-honored, two-volume yellow dictionary containing all those Latinate words. If words such as "abnegate," "exsiccate" or "stridulate" weren't in Harry's official dictionary, then Mom couldn't play them.

Stalemate!

And that was that. If Mom couldn't use the big yellow books, she wouldn't play Scrabble with Harry anymore. For his part, Harry vowed that if she wouldn't agree to use his much smaller, but very official, dictionary, he wouldn't play Scrabble with her, either.

Harry had carried the day, but his victory turned out to be a Pyrrhic one. Family lore holds that Mom and Uncle Harry, each as obstinate as the other, never played Scrabble with each other after that.

Harry died in November 2013. Mom died three months later.

As for the two-volume dictionary, it disappeared decades ago.

'Hello, mayor!' the prisoner said in greeting an inmate

THE GATE OF THE federal prison clanged shut behind me. I knew I was only going to be inside the Lewisburg penitentiary for a few hours. Even so, the sound of the gate closing triggered a mild nervous response.

In those days, I was a reporter for *The Daily Item*, a newspaper in Sunbury, Pennsylvania, and I had visited the prison several times previously – once to interview the warden and other times to cover special inmate events. On one of these occasions, Gov. Milton J. Shapp was the special guest of honor, and by coincidence I arrived at the gate just as the governor did. Two aides accompanied him, and we all went in – and came out – together.

During the summer of 1972, I belonged to the Sunbury Toastmasters Club, which fostered the art of public speaking.

Members of our club and the Williamsport Toastmasters were invited to a special dinner meeting near Lewisburg that was hosted by the Buffalo Valley Toastmasters Club. The three clubs were gathering to hold a speech contest. Since only inmates at Lewisburg could belong to the Buffalo Valley club, it was logical that the meeting would take place inside the prison.

Learning public speaking skills could be valuable to an inmate who wanted to improve himself. Speaking effectively would help during court proceedings, in appearances before the parole board, and in job interviews.

The dinner took place one evening in late summer. After we passed through the gate, the Toastmasters from Sunbury and Williamsport were escorted to a dining room in the main prison. Small tables were arranged around the room, with four chairs at each table. Up front, someone had put a lectern on a stand. This was appropriate since we had come for an evening of speeches.

Members of the Buffalo Valley club hadn't yet entered the dining room, and one of the prison officials, acting as our host, placed two of the visiting Toastmasters at each table. That way, each table would have two inmates and two visitors.

We had been seated for a short time when the prisoners entered the hall and walked over to the tables. Wearing khaki uniforms with short sleeves, they were smiling, obviously pleased to see us. Although I was a newsman, I was there on my own time and took no notes.

Two middle-aged men came up to our table, introduced themselves by first names – Ralph and Hugh – and sat down.

Ralph was a tall, thin man with dark hair. Hugh was heavyset and bald. Both were pleasant, and Ralph and I quickly got into a conversation.

As we talked, out of the corner of my eye, I saw that as other inmates passed our table, they were all greeting Hugh.

"Hello, mayor." one said.

"How are you, mayor?" another asked.

Hugh replied cordially to everyone.

Ralph noticed that I was watching and said, "He was Mayor Addonizio. I was his director of public works."

Hugh Addonizio (1914-1981) had been the mayor of Newark, N.J., before the U.S. Attorney for New Jersey successfully prosecuted him and other members of his administration on corruption charges.

I had lived in New Jersey then and had followed Addonizio's case very closely. I told that to Ralph, and soon Ralph, Hugh and I were having an animated, good-natured discussion about their trial.

We also talked a bit about another well-known inmate from New Jersey, also a politician.

"He's doing hard time," Hugh confided. "He sits in his cell and sulks. He won't talk to other prisoners."

That clearly wasn't Hugh's style, and he declared that this was no way to survive a prison term.

As for himself, Hugh said that on the day he surrendered to federal marshals to begin his prison term, he made a farewell speech to his political supporters and friends in Newark.

"I thought that was the last speech I was ever going to give," Hugh said.

But when he arrived at Lewisburg, prison officials encouraged him to join the Toastmasters Club and help other inmates sharpen their speaking skills.

When Hugh found out that I was one of three contestants in the humorous speech contest, he eagerly gave me some pointers.

My topic was about being left-handed. Armed with his encouragement and advice, I went on to win the contest.

Four decades have passed since that summer evening. I never saw Hugh again, but I retain the lessons the affable inmate inadvertently taught me:

Don't let adversity get you down. Whatever your situation, make the best of it. Don't brood. Don't sulk. Be cheerful. Help others.

Enough mischief left for one last Halloween

AS HALLOWEEN approached in 1989, David was dying. His doctors knew it. His mother and I knew it, and he knew it. His cancer had returned, and there was little anyone could do.

Once robust and active, David was twelve. Four years of treatment for malignant brain tumors had left him frail and thin. Surgeries, radiation and chemotherapy might have sapped his strength, but hadn't weakened his mischievous spirit.

By early October, David realized he would be too infirm to go door-to-door trick or treating, so he decided to get a spooky costume and sit quietly on a chair on the front porch. When children came up for their treats, they'd mistake David for just another Halloween dummy, but he planned to jerk and shriek and scare the daylights out of them.

Long before Halloween, he began shopping for just the right costume. Every weekend, Jane and I would take him to all the shops that sold Halloween stuff. Nothing satisfied him. Weeks passed, and we cautioned him that if he waited too long, all the good costumes would be gone. That didn't deter him. If a mask or a costume wasn't exactly what he wanted, he wouldn't buy it.

It was late in October when he found the perfect mask – an ugly skull capped by shaggy black hair.

The mask and hair covered David's entire head. He loved it, but we had doubts. After all, a grotesque death's head mask was hardly appropriate for a dying boy.

We pointed out that $25 was a lot of money to pay for a mask.

"It's my money," David said. "I want it."

We bought it. Then he selected a black cape that wrapped around his entire body. That cost $14.

David was delighted with his purchases. He'd be able to sit still, looking just like a front-porch dummy and then scream and wave his arms when costumed kids came up for their candy.

He got the mask and cape on the Saturday before Halloween, which was the following Wednesday.

On Sunday night, we were sitting on the couch watching TV, and David suddenly, urgently, asked me whether I would pay him $39 if he missed Halloween. I was surprised to see he was crying.

"Why would you miss Halloween?" I asked.

Tearfully, he explained that his physician, a pediatric oncologist, had scheduled him to come to the clinic on Wednesday afternoon for a treatment. Going for a treatment often involved getting a sedative, which David referred to as "getting zonked."

"If I get zonked, I'll be so sleepy I'll miss Halloween," he said.

"You'll be fine," I said, trying to reassure him.

As usual, I went to work on Monday morning. When I came home for lunch, David implored me to call his physician and reschedule his Wednesday appointment.

I called, but the doctor was busy. I left my work number so he could call me at the office. I ate lunch and tried unsuccessfully to cheer up a morose child.

I hadn't been back at work very long when the telephone rang. It was the doctor, and he was laughing. He said he had called the house just after I left.

David had taken the call and explained his position in language that the doctor understood: "If you zonk me and I miss Halloween, I'm going to sue you for $39. That's what my costume cost."

Chuckling, the oncologist told me that he had quickly backed down. Of course, David could come to the clinic on the day after Halloween.

On Halloween, trick-or-treating began after supper. David suited up happily. He was strong enough to go house-to-house, at least for a while, and he and his mother started down the street.

When neighbors realized who the child was underneath that hideous mask with all that shaggy black hair, they gave him double and triple the treats that everybody else got.

David was able to go to a dozen houses. When he came home, he was tired but happy.

The next afternoon, when he and his mother went to the clinic for his rescheduled appointment, he took his bag of goodies and shared them with the other children. He made sure that his doctor got some, too.

That was many Halloweens ago. As we had feared, it became David's last Halloween. He died three months later.

On trick-or-treat night for years after that, I put David's grotesque mask on a dummy on the front porch, in my son's phrase, "just to scare kids." But the mask melted one hot summer, and I've never found another one quite as ugly.

At Halloween, I still put dummies on the porch. They will sit on a rocking chair and wear black trousers, black sweatshirt and black boots. The head? A large plastic skull, topped by a big black hat.

I'm sure of two things: A.) Some children will be frightened. B.) David would approve.

A visit to the Va. battlefield where my Civil War ancestor died

IN THE POPULAR Civil War song, the crowd shouts "Hurrah! Hurrah!" when Johnny comes marching home. Unlike Johnny, my ancestor – 19-year-old Anderson Pidcock – didn't survive the war.

The first cousin of my father's grandmother, Anderson enlisted in the Union army in August 1861, shortly after the Confederates routed the Northern soldiers at the Battle of Bull Run in Virginia. The apprentice carpenter was sixteen. For nearly three years, he fought as a member of the Sixth New Jersey Infantry Volunteers, first as a private and then as a corporal. He died – "killed in action" – down South in 1864.

During the war's sesquicentennial, I decided to visit the battlefield where he fell, so one sunny weekend in September 2013, a friend and I traveled to northern Virginia to a place called The Wilderness. In May 1864, some 62,000 Southern soldiers commanded by General Robert E. Lee clashed with 120,000 Northern soldiers led by Lieutenant General U.S. Grant. Two days of fighting occurred there.

The battlefield is about 20 miles west of Fredericksburg, Virginia It was – and is – an immense tract of woods and swamps. Although developments of residential and retail complexes now cover much of it, the National Park Service has preserved significant sections of The Wilderness.

The two days of fighting here began on Thursday, May 5, 1864, when Union troops clashed with Confederates along a road called the Orange Turnpike. Lee ordered more Southern forces into the battle to halt the Union advance on Richmond, about 70 miles away.

Fighting resumed early on the morning of Friday, May 6. Union soldiers in General Winfield Scott Hancock's II Corps attacked General A.P. Hill's division of Confederates at 5 a.m. The charge took place to the south of the Orange Plank Road, just west of its intersection with Brock Road.

Anderson's regiment was up front. "He's in the second line going forward," Park Ranger Beth Parnicza told us as she looked at a map that showed the location and movements of specific units on that fateful day. "He's going to be in the thick of everything."

The battle raged, then slowed. In late morning the Confederates mounted a counterattack: 4,000 rebel soldiers under General James Longstreet moved east along an unfinished railroad line that let them go around the side of Hancock's force.

"The Sixth New Jersey would have borne much of the weight of Longstreet's flank attack at 11 a.m., but perhaps not the brunt of the attack, since they were not on the end," the ranger said. The soldiers in "the regiment would have found themselves struggling to hold their ground in such a situation and probably would have been swept up in the attack."

At some point, Anderson was killed.

Around 4 in the afternoon, Lee ordered a major attack on Hancock's line along Brock Road, and the offensive hit Pidcock's regiment "He's probably fallen by then . . . He's really in the thick of a lot of it," Parnicza said.

This section of The Wilderness caught fire that day. Sparks from soldiers' campfire and flames from the barrels of thousands of muskets set the brush and dry leaves afire. According to the ranger, the fires had begun "during the Confederate assault, and the wind blew the fire back into the faces of the Union forces . . . It is definitely something your ancestor faced if he was still on the line at that time."

By coincidence, Anderson's distant cousin Hiram Pidcoe from Williamsport, Pennsylvania, was also fighting in this section of The Wilderness. Pidcoe, who survived the war, belonged to the First Pennsylvania Light Artillery. The two cousins likely didn't know each other. Pidcoe wrote about this battle in his journal, which a descendant recently published, but his entry for this battle doesn't mention meeting up with Pidcock.

Parnicza and another ranger gave us directions that let us find the place where the Sixth New Jersey had fought that day. It remains heavily wooded. My friend and I walked through the trees and brush where the fighting occurred. There were few other visitors that afternoon, and our feet made little noise as we followed a path maintained by the park service. I remember the occasional chirping of birds and the sounds of cars and pickup trucks driving along Brock and Orange Plank roads nearby, but otherwise, the woods were quiet. Along Brock Road we saw the remains of hurriedly dug trenches that Hancock's men had made.

In terms of statistics, The Battle of The Wilderness resulted in 26,000 casualties, a figure that includes both dead and wounded. Of these, 8,000 were Confederate soldiers, and 18,000 were Union men.

Many soldiers who died there were buried in the Fredericksburg National Cemetery after the war, but Anderson Pidcock's name doesn't appear on the cemetery's roster. The New Jersey cemetery where his stone is located wasn't established until 1878, and its records don't list burials.

I don't know where Anderson Pidcock was buried. I learned in Virginia that the bodies of hundreds of soldiers who perished at The Wilderness were never identified. It's possible that Anderson was one of these unknown soldiers.

Be that as it may, the fighting at the Wilderness had slowed, but not stopped Grant. On Saturday, May 7 – the day after Anderson Pidcock died – the general resumed his march toward Richmond. When his soldiers realized they were heading south, they cheered.

Civil War ancestor guarded Va. railroad used to supply Union troops

IN SEPTEMBER 1864, my grandfather's grandfather, then a raw recruit in the Union Army, traveled from Pittsburgh, Pennsylvania, to northern Virginia, where he guarded a railroad line that crossed guerrilla-infested Confederate territory.

Born in 1837, his name was Frederick Bennett. He was 27, married, a father, and a resident of Allegheny County when he enlisted on August 31, 1864, in the 212th Pennsylvania Volunteers, which was organized at Camp Reynolds near Pittsburgh, on September 15.

To learn about Bennett's time in the service, 150 years later I traveled south of the Mason-Dixon Line to find out about military events that were relevant to his service along the Virginia rail line in late September, October and November of 1864. Over three days, a friend and I visited Harper's Ferry, West Virginia; and, traveling on to northern Virginia, stopped at Winchester and Strasburg; and explored the Cedar Creek battlefield, where federal troops won a crucial victory.

Here are highlights of what I learned:

Bennett served less than 10 months. Of these, he spent two months guarding the Orange and Alexandria Railroad, which was used to supply the Federal Army that in late 1864 laid waste to Virginia's Shenandoah Valley. The line ran through

Manassas, about 30 miles southwest of Washington, D.C.

It's likely that his regiment traveled by train for its initial deployment in Washington City. It's possible that the troops took the Pennsylvania Railroad and went by way of Harrisburg, but it's also possible that they took the Baltimore & Ohio Railroad. If so, they passed Harper's Ferry, an important military center at the confluence of the Potomac and Shenandoah rivers.

Lieutenant General U.S. Grant spent the night of September 16 in Harper's Ferry, staying in a two-story, red-brick building. Earlier that day, Grant had met with General Phillip Sheridan in nearby Charles Town, West Virginia, to discuss Sheridan's upcoming Shenandoah Campaign.

Grant wanted Sheridan to destroy the Confederate forces led by General Jubal Early who then controlled the Shenandoah Valley. Frederick Bennett and his comrades in the 212th Pennsylvania were to play a very minor supporting role in this campaign.

By September 17, the Pennsylvania regiment was on the move, heading for the U.S. capital. When the soldiers got there, they were assigned to a division belonging to the garrison of a network of 68 forts and batteries that protected the capital.

By September 29, the regiment was reassigned and sent across the Potomac to Virginia. As Samuel P. Bates reported in his 1871 reference book, *History of Pennsylvania Volunteers, 1861-65*, many of the soldiers of the 212th Pennsylvania had had prior military experience – my ancestor did not – and "the regiment was . . . ordered to duty in guarding the portion of the Orange and Alexandria Railroad lying between Alexandria and Manassas."

According to Bates: "Over this road, supplies for Sheridan's army were transported, and the regiment was charged with keeping open the part entrusted to it. It was an enemy's country and infested by roving bands, military or civil upon occasion, and to guard against surprise, and to be at all points superior to an attacking force, required incessant watchfulness and skill in the disposition and handling of the guards."

At one point, three soldiers belonging to the regiment ventured into the countryside, even though, as Bates said, "To go outside the lines was almost certain death." Southern guerillas caught the three in an ambush and shot them down. Then, "pistols in hand," they ran up to the bodies "and fired into their breasts until they were quite dead," Bates said.

At Manassas Junction, the Orange and Alexandria connected with the Manassas Gap Railroad, which, heading west toward the Shenandoah Valley, used a mountain pass called Manassas Gap to reach the Shenandoah's agricultural regions. Valley farmers provided the Confederates with much food, and Sheridan was determined to stop this.

Frequent fighting had inflicted significant damage on both railroads. As Sheridan saw it, one obstacle to keeping the line open from Front Royal to Alexandria was that of manpower. This "will require large guards to protect it against a small number of partisan troops," Sheridan said.

But Grant decided to repair and reopen the Orange and Alexandria as far west as Manassas Junction, then repair most of the Manassas Gap line. Clearly, Grant was anticipating a Union victory in the Shenandoah and already calculating the best and quickest way for Sheridan's troops to join the Army of the Potomac at Petersburg. With the railroad back in operation, Sheridan would be able to move his army rapidly across Virginia to Alexandria, where steamboats could quickly transport the soldiers down the Potomac to the Petersburg/Richmond theater.

At Winchester, a September 19 battle saw Sheridan's troops defeat Early's Confederates. In one key part of the fight, Confederate defenders at Fort Collier were overpowered by a Union cavalry charge led by a young general named George A. Custer.

A month later, as the Battle of Cedar Creek unfolded, fighting enveloped a country cemetery, swept across the village of Middletown, and swirled around a plantation called Belle Grove, where white columns still bear the scars of bullets fired during the fight.

Early's surprise attack along Cedar Creek had routed many of the federals, but Sheridan regrouped his men, and forced the Confederates to withdraw. The dramatic victory came weeks before Abraham Lincoln stood for re-election, and gave the president an important boost at the polls.

As Sheridan's Shenandoah campaign ended, he ordered his soldiers to burn all the valley's farms and mills. That way, the Confederates couldn't use its crops to feed rebel soldiers.

I haven't yet determined if Sheridan's men took the Manassas Gap Railroad when they left the Shenandoah, but a highlight of my weekend jaunt came when we located the present-day rail line as it comes through the mountains just east of Strasburg. This was close to the route of the Civil War railroad.

Farther east along the Orange and Alexandria line, it's doubtful that Private Frederick Bennett saw much, if any, action. As Bates reported in his book about the Pennsylvania volunteers:

"About the middle of November – Sheridan having in the meantime cleared the Shenandoah Valley of the foe – this line of railway was abandoned and the regiment was ordered back to the defenses of Washington, being posted at Forts Marcy, Ward, Craig, Reno, Albany, Lyon and others."

He added, "Previous to this time, it had been armed and drilled as infantry. It was now instructed in heavy artillery service."

The war ended in April 1865, and my ancestor was discharged on May 13. Bennett returned to Pittsburgh, where his wife and 6-year-old daughter (who eventually became my mother's grandmother) awaited him.

Confessions of a sometimes Santa

I'LL NEVER FORGET the first time I ever played Santa Claus. It was December 1972. I was a reporter for *The Daily Item*, the newspaper at Sunbury, Pennsylvania, and I did it for a story.

I borrowed a Santa costume; suited up in the newsroom; had a colleague adjust the beard; found my courage; and walked across Market Street to Santa's house in Cameron Park.

Eager children and smiling parents stood waiting by the house. "Here he comes!" someone shouted.

I climbed a step or two and sat in Santa's slightly elevated chair. The children started coming up to sit in Santa's lap and tell him what they wanted for Christmas.

Some, especially the little ones, came reluctantly. Others, especially the older ones, harbored suspicions. "Are you really Santa?" one boy asked.

A little girl got her tiny fingers in Santa's beard and tugged ever so gently.

It was a cool evening, and for two full hours, one by one, the children came up to Santa, many with eyes open wide and brimming with belief.

Predictably, girls wanted dolls, and boys wanted trucks or trains.

Invariably I asked each child: "Have you obeyed your mommy and your daddy all year?"

All but one said that they had. When I put the question to the tot who became the exception – a pretty little girl with brown eyes – she blurted out, "I don't have a daddy!"

Her mother gave Santa a furious look.

Late in the session, a man and woman arrived with three small children who came up one by one and confided their Christmas requests. As the third child got down, the man walked over and said quietly that the woman was his sister and that she was mentally challenged. Could she come up and sit on Santa's lap?

"Of course," I said.

Smiling, she settled happily into Santa's lap. As we chatted, I realized that although she was older than I was, she was as full of belief and excitement as any of the children who had preceded her.

As she left, she said, "Merry Christmas, Santa!"

"Merry Christmas," I replied. I tried to say it heartily, but I was feeling sad.

Over the years, I've learned that to succeed as a Santa, one needs to have all the correct elements of a costume and all the essential accessories. My own collection includes two sacks for toys, one green and one red; several pairs of old-fashioned spectacles; and three pairs of black boots, two of which have faux fur lining the tops.

I wasn't nearly so well equipped when, a few days before Christmas in 1975, I performed as Santa for the kindergarten class attended by our oldest child.

I felt fully confident as I bounded into the classroom, dressed in a borrowed suit and carrying a huge sack of presents over my shoulder.

"Merry Christmas, children," I exclaimed.

"Merry Christmas, Santa," the children said.

Suddenly a little boy shouted out, "Hey! That's my dad!" He happened to be my son.

As the other children lined up for a quick chat with Santa, the teacher took my boy aside. "Why do you think that's your father," she asked.

"My dad has shoes like that," he replied.

Nothing the teacher said could persuade him otherwise. When it was my son's turn to sit on Santa's lap, he smiled and asked, "Where'd you get the suit, Dad?"

"Shhh," I said. "I'm here on special assignment from the North Pole."

To be sure, he had spotted a flaw. I was wearing black tie shoes beneath black spats that rose nearly to my knees. The next time I played Santa, I wore a pair of shiny black boots.

On occasion, I have dressed as Santa Claus and gone to the homes of friends.

One recent Christmas Eve, I put on my Santa suit and carried an assortment of wrapped and beribboned presents to the neighbors who live next door. Mrs. Claus had even arranged for Santa's pack to contain something for the neighbors' dog, a large and energetic German Shepherd.

When Santa arrived, the dog was in the backyard, but as I pulled the doggy treat out of the pack, some well-meaning person opened the backdoor so the pooch could come in for his gift.

The dog rushed into the kitchen, but stopped abruptly when he spotted a white-bearded man in a bright red suit and white gloves standing in the next room. First he barked. Then he charged.

Not to worry. Santa pointed his gloved index finger right at the dog's eyes. In a loud, firm voice, Santa commanded, "SIT!"

The dog sat. Crisis averted.

After all, nobody misbehaves on Christmas Eve.